REHABILITATI

Over the last two decades empirical evidence has increasingly supported the view that it is possible to reduce reoffending rates by rehabilitating offenders rather than simply punishing them. In fact, the pendulum's swing back from a pure punishment model to a rehabilitation model is arguably one of the most significant events in modern correctional policy. This comprehensive review argues that rehabilitation should focus on promoting human goods (i.e. providing the offender with the essential ingredients for a "good" life) as well as on reducing or avoiding risk.

Providing a succinct summary and critique of the scientific approach to offender rehabilitation, this intriguing volume for students of criminology, sociology and clinical psychology gives a comprehensive evaluation of both the Risk–Need–Responsivity Model and the Good Lives Model.

Rehabilitation is a value-laden process involving a delicate balance of the needs and desires of clinicians, clients, the State and the public. Written by two internationally renowned academics in rehabilitation research, this book argues that intervention with offenders is not simply a matter of implementing the best therapeutic technology and leaving political and social debate to politicians and policy-makers.

Tony Ward is Professor of Clinical Psychology and Clinical Director at Victoria University of Wellington, New Zealand. His research interests include the offence process in offenders, cognitive distortions and models of rehabilitation. He has published over 190 research articles, chapters and books.

Shadd Maruna is a reader in Criminology at Queen's University Belfast. Previously he has been a lecturer at the University of Cambridge and the State University of New York. His previous book, *Making Good: How Ex-Convicts Reform and Rebuild Their Lives* (2001) was named the Outstanding Contribution to Criminology by the American Society of Criminology in 2001.

KEY IDEAS IN CRIMINOLOGY

SERIES EDITOR: TIM NEWBURN, MANNHEIM CENTRE FOR CRIMINOLOGY, LONDON SCHOOL OF ECONOMICS

Key Ideas in Criminology explores the major concepts, issues, debates and controversies in criminology. The series aims to provide authoritative essays on central topics within the broader area of criminology. Each book adopts a strong individual "line", constituting an original essay rather than a literature survey, and offers a lively and agenda-setting treatment of its subject matter.

These books will appeal to students, teachers and researchers in criminology, sociology, social policy, cultural studies, law and political science.

Series editor Tim Newburn is Professor of Criminology and Social Policy, Director of the Mannheim Centre for Criminology, London School of Economics, and President of the British Society of Criminology. He has written and researched widely on issues of crime and justice.

Forthcoming in the series:

Penal Populism
JOHN PRATT

Rehabilitation
TONY WARD and
SHADD MARUNA

Security
LUCIA ZEDNER

Surveillance
BENJAMIN GOOLD

Feminist Criminology
CLAIRE RENZETTI

Victims
PAUL ROCK

Policing
MICHAEL KEMPA and
CLIFFORD SHEARING

REHABILITATION
Beyond the risk paradigm

TONY WARD and SHADD MARUNA

Routledge
Taylor & Francis Group

LONDON AND NEW YORK

HV
9275
.W36
2007

First published 2007
by Routledge
2 Park Square, Milton Park, Abingdon, Oxon OX14 4RN

Simultaneously published in the USA and Canada
by Routledge
270 Madison Ave, New York, NY 10016

Routledge is an imprint of the Taylor & Francis Group, an informa business

© 2007 Tony Ward and Shadd Maruna

Typeset in Garamond 3 by
RefineCatch Limited, Bungay, Suffolk
Printed and bound in Great Britain by
TJ International Ltd, Padstow, Cornwall

British Library Cataloguing in Publication Data
A catalogue record for this book is available from the British Library

Library of Congress Cataloging in Publication Data
A catalog record for this book has been requested

ISBN 10: 0–415–38643–8 (pbk)
ISBN 10: 0–415–38642–X (hbk)
ISBN 10: 0–203–96217–6 (ebk)

ISBN 13: 978–0–415–38643–2 (pbk)
ISBN 13: 978–0–415–38642–5 (hbk)
ISBN 13: 978–0–203–96217–6 (ebk)

For my sisters Joy Creet and Donna Ward
    TW

For Nick, who could teach the likes of me a thing or two about rehabilitation
    SM

CONTENTS

LIST OF FIGURES

ACKNOWLEDGMENTS

The ideas in this book have been developed over the past decade in collaboration with a number of close colleagues and co-authors, in particular: Gordon Bazemore, Tony Beech, Dawn Fisher, Mark Brown, Ros Burnett, Sharon Casey, Tim Chapman, Rachael Collie, Andy Day, Lynne Eccleston, Theresa Gannon, Clive Hollin, Mary McMurran, Kevin Howells, Steve Hudson, Richard Laws, Richard Siegert, Thomas P. LeBel, Alison Liebling, Ruth Mann, Bill Marshall, Joe Melser, Nick Mitchell, Michelle Naples, Emma Palmer, Mayumi Purvis, Claire Stewart, Jim Vess, Carolyn Wilshire and Pamela Yates. They all share an equal part of the credit for the useful contributions of this book, but none of the blame for its shortcomings and mistakes. Special thanks go to Hans Toch for the idea of writing this book and for many of the insights within it. He is magnanimous enough to accept both flaws and credits in the work, so all hate mail should go to him. Our gratitude goes to David Wexler for bringing both of us together a few years ago. David thought that our different research programs had something important in common. He was right! We also want to thank Lo Presser and Lila Kazemian for being kind enough to proofread several very rough drafts for us and for providing extremely helpful suggestions for change. Thanks to Tim Newburn for encouraging us to write this for the Key Ideas in Criminology series and to Routledge (and our families!) for their undying patience as we struggled along with it. Research assistance was generously provided by Joe Melser and Roisin Devlin.

Importantly, a word of acknowledgment has to go to the group of scholars with whom we are in dialogue in this book. They go by many names and most will know who they are without us naming them. Sometimes they are called the "What Works" group, or the "New Rehabilitationists", but most often they are just referred to as "the Canadians" (even though their numbers include representation from nearly every continent). In this book, we shall refer to them as the individuals behind the Risk–Need–Responsivity (RNR) Model of rehabilitation. They have been the most influential and important voice of support for evidenced-based correctional policy (as opposed to penal populism or punitive retributivism) for the past thirty years. They have even been credited with "saving" rehabilitation from a premature death. For this alone, they deserve enormous thanks. What they have achieved has required intellectual courage, painstaking precision, stamina, creativity, rigor and perseverance. Lots of us believe in rehabilitation as an ideal and as a science – indeed, public opinion polls suggest the majority of the public share these views with those of us in the criminology business – but the RNR academics have been a lone voice in terms of providing a *theory* for how rehabilitation can and should work. Who else has stuck their neck out and actually developed a testable and comprehensive model like the RNR? The rest of us do a lot of talking and sometimes throw around criticisms of rehabilitation practice – it isn't sensitive enough to race and gender issues, it is too narrow, and so on – but we don't tend to offer any serious alternatives.

Playing the critic is far easier than doing what the RNR theorists have done. Their model is internally consistent, compelling, and based on an impressive foundation of empirical research (see MacKenzie, 2006; McGuire, 2004). It is also, of course, imperfect, which is where this book begins. Yet our ambition is not simply to throw stones. Neither of the authors is confrontational by nature, and neither of us believes in engaging in academic squabbles simply for the sake of it.

The RNR model is explicitly dynamic in nature, and none of the RNR theorists has ever claimed that RNR was the last word in rehabilitation theory. Indeed, very much to their credit as scholars and scientists, RNR theorists have welcomed "skepticisms, indeed 'unsparing criticism' " of their work (Andrews, Bonta and Wormith, 2006, p. 22). In fact, they have explicitly welcomed our own criticisms regarding the negativity of the RNR model and the over-emphasis on risks (to the exclusion of strengths): "We strongly endorse explorations of the issues surrounding RNR and other principles. The idea of enhancing RNR through greater attention to human motivation is very attractive" (Andrews *et al.*, 2006, p. 22). It is with this extremely generous invitation in mind that we pursue the arguments in this book. Our sole hope, like that of the RNR theorists, is that this book can lead to an improvement in the quality of offender rehabilitation practices.

As our final word of acknowledgment, then, we want to thank our friends, the RNR theorists and advocates – in *advance* – for accepting this book as a complement and, indeed, a compliment to their important work and not as some mean-spirited attack. May we work together to help rehabilitation theory develop and grow.

1

HOW DID "REHABILITATION" BECOME A DIRTY WORD?

> No one but an academic simpleton will even use the word "rehabilitation" without apprehension.
>
> Richard Korn (1992, p. 4)

There are not many subjects as sexy as criminology and criminological psychology. Step into a taxi, sit down for a haircut, or get chatting to a stranger on an airplane, and when you are asked, "So what do you do?" try responding: "I'm a psychologist who studies crime." Watch their eyes light up. Getting inside the mind of the serial killer? Assisting police officers on their toughest cases? Outsmarting the smartest criminal masterminds? People love that stuff! Even the more mundane areas of criminology – prisons, prostitution, corporate crime, cop culture, gangs, sexual violence, political economy of crime, heroin markets – are all fascinating stuff.

But wait for the follow-up question, "What sort of research?" and try answering: "Offender rehabilitation." First, there is a pause (always a pause), sometimes for a few seconds, sometimes for as many as ten or fifteen. They know the phrase, but it has been a while since they last heard it.

Offender rehabilitation? Then you will get the inevitable reply: "H'm, bet it doesn't work, does it?" And, no matter what you respond, the conversation will quickly turn to the weather or sport. At best you will get a "Well, good luck to ya, mate", which is frequently followed by a mumbled "Better you than me".

Indeed, offender rehabilitation has to be the single least-sexy topic within the broad umbrella of criminological research. Undergraduates who flock to courses on the "psychology of crime" will turn and run with equal speed away from a course titled "psychology of criminal reform". Mention the topic to book publishers, faculty colleagues, aspiring PhDs, and watch the yawns and the attempts to escape the room without being rude.

The whole idea behind rehabilitation, let alone the word itself, has a musty, anachronistic quality to it, belonging to another era when society shared a sense of the "right" way to live (and, indeed, a "wrong" way as well). Who has the right to tell others how they should live? How dare some middle-class clinician lecture a group of disadvantaged, ghetto-dwelling youth about right and wrong? If someone wants to break the law, that is their choice, isn't it? If they want to do the crime, they can do the time. Who needs the moral hand-wringing and condescension?

Indeed, there is something vaguely preachy and evangelical about the notion of rehabilitation. After all, who goes around saving sinners any more? To many of us, "rehabilitation" has become synonymous with workbook-centered lectures delivered in grim, windowless prison basements: tiresome bureaucratic exercises that are as meaningless to participants as they are to staff administering them. Nothing more than a way to tick a box (rehabilitation? check) and pass some dead time during the long years of incarceration. Others hear the word and associate it with an extreme "medical model" view of corrections. Borrowed as it is from the wider medical literature, the term "rehabilitation" invokes, for many, images of clinicians in white lab-coats surgically rewiring bad brains into good. Finally, to some, the word conjures the sexist image of "Sally Social Worker": soft, gullible, heart in the right place, but dangerously naïve. Time to wake up to reality, Sally, this is 2007, not 1957. The world has changed. Crime has changed. Offenders have changed. Who needs a book about an embarrassing old relic like rehabilitation in 2007?

Now, "reentry", on the other hand – there's an interesting topic! The reentry of prisoners into the community is a different subject altogether. Ever since Jeremy Travis (2000) famously warned that "they all come back", the criminological world has been feverishly pursuing this "new" topic of ex-prisoner reentry. In a ten-page document, the then director of the National Institute of Justice (NIJ) described the scale of the reentry project in the United States in clear terms and outlined how little attention the subject had received despite its potentially central role in community safety and recidivism reduction:

> The explosive, continuing growth of the Nation's prison population is a well-known fact. . . . Less well recognized is one of the consequences of this extraordinarily high figure. . . . If current trends continue, this year more than half a million people will leave prison and return to neighborhoods across the country.
>
> (Travis, 2000: 1)

In other words, if you lock 2 million people up in jails, as the United States has done, you are going to create an enormous number of ex-convicts, so you had better be prepared (as had they). In all, it was a fairly unremarkable observation really. Yet the reaction among policy-makers, criminologists and research foundations internationally has been nothing short of amazing. Since the NIJ published this call to arms, there have been literally countless conferences, commissions, reports, articles, books, research projects and government initiatives launched around the issue of returning ex-prisoners in the US (for reviews, see Maruna and LeBel, 2003; Petersilia, 2003; Travis, 2005), culminating in the remarkably weighty 650-page *Report of the Re-entry Policy Council* (Re-entry Policy Council, 2005).

As is often the case (see Newburn, 2002), there have been parallel developments around resettlement in the United Kingdom over the last decade, with numerous new reports and commissions of equal importance (see especially Morgan and Owers, 2001; Social Exclusion Unit, 2001). In the United Kingdom, however, "resettlement" rather than "re-entry" has become the buzzword of choice. John Braithwaite (1989) popularized the longstanding notion of "reintegration" in his landmark book, *Crime, Shame and Reintegration*. Even "recovery" has become a term in vogue, spreading out from the addiction and mental-health literature to the criminal justice world more broadly (see especially Draine *et al.*, 2006). This makes perfect sense considering the high proportion of those under criminal-justice supervision who also struggle with issues of addiction, mental illness and substance abuse. Finally, academic criminologists have started using the awkward term "desistance from crime" to describe the process of "going straight" or self-reform. Although the word, somewhat oddly, does not start with "re-", desistance has become one of the most popular topics in criminological journals and books in recent years (see, e.g., Farrall and Calverley, 2006; Laub and Sampson, 2001).

So why title a book *Rehabilitation* when so many newer, shinier terms are available to choose from? We have no specific interest in resurrecting this particular word, especially as it has sadly become anathema to prisoners and probationers. At the same time, we worry about disguising old ideas and practices in new terminology, old wine in new bottles. Listen, for instance, to this definition of resettlement provided by the UK Association of Chief Officers of Probation:

> A systematic and evidenced-based process by which actions are taken to work with the offender in custody and on release, so that communities are better protected from harm and re-offending is significantly reduced. It encompasses the totality of work with prisoners, their families and significant others in partnership with statutory and voluntary organisations.
>
> (Cited in Morgan and Owers, 2001: 12)

How is this in any way different from what used to be called rehabilitation? Likewise, the word "reentry" is hardly ever defined (Lynch, 2006) and appears to have been chosen as the "buzzword" of the moment (Austin, 2001) almost entirely on the basis of its lack of connotations (Maruna, 2006).

The situation is marginally better for the more traditional term "rehabilitation" (see Raynor and Robinson, 2005, for a comprehensive review of definitions of rehabilitation in the criminological literature and beyond). In their article "Recent advances in rehabilitation" in the *British Medical Journal*, Wade and de Jong (2000) acknowledge that "a definition of rehabilitation has still not been universally agreed" in the medical profession but offer the following as the closest thing to the reigning usage of the word:

> Rehabilitation is a reiterative, active, educational, problem solving process focused on a patient's behavior (disability), with the following components:
>
> • Assessment – the identification of the nature and extent of the patient's problems and the factors relevant to their resolution

- Goal setting
- Intervention, which may include either or both of
  (a) treatments, which affect the process of change;
  (b) support, which maintains the patient's quality of life
  and his or her safety
- Evaluation – to check on the effects of any intervention

This definition does not translate perfectly into the criminal justice arena. In particular, the term "treatment", although widely used in the criminological literature, will sound awkward to the average probationer or prisoner. Unless they are enrolled in a methadone maintenance program or are receiving medication for a mental illness, few such individuals will feel they are undergoing any "treatment". Yet the same can be said for many forms of therapeutic intervention (see Schneider, 1999). Besides, the word "treatment" has another, more generic usage, along the lines of "Describe your overall treatment by prison or probation staff". If understood in this sense – or simply as a "relationship" as urged by Schneider (1999) – the above definition seems a perfectly adequate, open-ended description of the practices we call rehabilitation and others have rebranded as resettlement, reentry, reintegration, aftercare, and so forth.[1]

Part of the purpose of rebranding is to throw off the "baggage" and reputation that came with the previous name. So, for instance, in Northern Ireland, the badly maligned Royal Ulster Constabulary (RUC) was rechristened the Police Service of Northern Ireland in an attempt to move on from the past into a new kind of future (see Mulcahy, 2006). The problem, as made obvious in the Northern Ireland example, is that it is far easier to rename an agency than to change entrenched bureaucratic cultures and practices. Indeed, one of the dangerous things about making up new words, as Stanley Cohen (1985, p. 152) points out, is the way new terminology gives the illusion of progress even when "much the same groups of experts are doing much the same business as usual".

Changing names is also a poor way of preserving and learning from the past. For instance, judging only by the name (as one might reasonably do in this era of "key word" searches), "reentry" appears to have a fairly short history. The writer of a journal article on the topic can (and many do) put together a reasonably comprehensive literature review on the topic by summarizing the book-jacket copy of recent works by Travis (2005) and Joan Petersilia (2003). Rehabilitation, on the other hand, has a long, well-known and well-documented history. This history (or "baggage") is not always pretty – in fact, it can be fairly characterized as consistently disappointing – yet it is crucial to acknowledge and learn from these dramatic experiences in order to develop better practice, and not just reinvent a broken wheel. Although this book will not attempt to review the history of rehabilitation endeavors in any way, there are numerous sources one can consult in this regard (see, e.g., Garland, 2001; Morris and Rothman, 1995; Raynor and Robinson, 2005; for addiction treatment, see especially White, 1998).

Maybe more than any other area of criminological research, rehabilitation has been plagued with new discoveries, miracle cures, revolutions and silver bullets, all buffeted by that all-powerful justification of "science" (see Cohen, 1985; Mair, 2004). Ours, on the other hand, is a rather unabashedly "old school" approach to this topic, as will be seen in later chapters. We seek to return to basics in some ways, recasting rehabilitation as a way of helping people who want to go straight. As such, we decided, after much consideration, that the old-fashioned term "rehabilitation" will suit our discussion just fine.

WWIII: THE THIRD COMING OF THE "WHAT WORKS" DEBATE

Now on to the next order of business: This rehabilitation stuff doesn't really *work*, does it?

No self-respecting book on rehabilitation begins without a poke at a straw man named Robert Martinson. In his infamous 1974 article titled "What Works", Martinson implied (and later stated) that the answer, when it comes to offender rehabilitation, is "nothing". In doing so, Martinson created one of academia's most remarkable legacies, the most painful aspect of which is that every article, chapter or book written on the subject of rehabilitation since 1974 has had to start by first knocking Dr Martinson down. Indeed, the history of rehabilitation, told so often, always follows the same classic arch; it is the great story of the rise and fall and rise again (redemption at last!) of the rehabilitative ideal.

Everyone knows this tune, so feel free to sing along. First, there was the *Good Old Days* when everyone believed in rehabilitation and prisons were about correction and reform. The ideal of rehabilitation possibly reached a sort of peak in California in the late 1960s and early 1970s when the state invested in both highly innovative, theoretically sound interventions with young people and the research needed to evaluate and improve these practices (see, e.g., Cressey, 1958; Palmer, 1975; Warren, 1969; but see Irwin, 1974, for the perspective of an ex-prisoner criminologist). Then came the *Fall from Grace* (or "California research at the crossroads" as Martinson [1976] labeled it). The Martinson Report was just one among a series of critiques from the political Left, Right and Center that helped to usher in an era of "nothing works" pessimism and "lock 'em up" punitiveness. Yet it should not be forgotten, as Garland (2001) convincingly argues, that these critiques alone cannot be blamed for the punitive turn. The War on Crime, the War on Drugs, "Prison Works" and the unbelievable escalation of prisoner numbers in the US and elsewhere were the product of discernible structural and cultural shifts in the social landscape. But Martinson's report (and others like it) surely didn't help things much.

But no need to despair. A hero was on the way – twelve of them, to be specific! – mainly blowing in from Canada and ushering in a new golden age of rehabilitative initiatives. A group of researchers and practitioners were labeled with the shorthand tag of the *"What Works" Movement*, self-consciously although somewhat ironically taking their name from Martinson's notorious article. The evidence assembled by these "What Works" researchers was massive, sophisticated and seemingly incontrovertible (see, e.g., Andrews and Dowden, 2005; Lipsey, 1992; Redondo, Sanchez-Meca and Garrido, 2002). First we got meta-analyses, then we had meta-analyses of meta-analyses. In short, it was a campaign of "shock and awe" that seemed to end the thirty-year reign of skepticism following Martinson's flawed, over-exposed and exaggerated review (for a review, see Gendreau, 1981; Palmer, 1975).

Indeed, in 2004, with an audience of nearly a thousand criminologists from around the globe, the President of the American Society of Criminology, Frank Cullen, symbolically tore down criminology's statue of Robert Martinson for ever. In a talk, immodestly titled "The twelve people who saved rehabilitation: How the science of criminology made a difference", Cullen announced that victory was, at last, in hand and that the Good Guys had won:

Three decades ago, it was widely believed by criminologists and policymakers that "nothing works" to reform offenders and that "rehabilitation is dead" as a guiding correctional philosophy. By contrast, today there is a vibrant movement to reaffirm rehabilitation and to implement programs based on the principles of effective intervention. How did this happen? I contend that the saving of rehabilitation was a contingent reality that emerged due to the efforts of a small group of loosely coupled research criminologists. These scholars rejected the "nothing works" professional ideology and instead used rigorous science to show that popular punitive interventions were ineffective, that offenders were not beyond redemption, and that treatment programs rooted in criminological knowledge were capable of meaningfully reducing recidivism.

(Cullen, 2005)

Unquestionably, Cullen was right; the past decade has witnessed something of a rehabilitation renaissance. In what Pallone and Hennessy (2003) describe as the "Rebellion of 2000", California voters passed Proposition 36 requiring sentences of community-based drug treatment – not jail time – for most nonviolent drug offenders. In fact, the state that once removed the word "rehabilitation" from its constitution (Petersilia, 2003) actually rebranded its Department of Corrections with the bizarrely repetitive new name the California Department of Corrections and Rehabilitation. (See the warning above about new names for old practices, but this appears to be more than window dressing.) According to the *Christian Science Monitor* (May 27 2005), "After decades of tough policies, America's most-populous state is poised to reverse direction in its approach to the incarceration of youth – from punishment to rehabilitation".

Yet the story of rehabilitation is not exactly over. No sooner was Cullen's presidential address published than along came the anachronistic sight of a slim book called *Rethinking Rehabilitation: Why Can't We Reform Our Criminals?* In the book, published by the American Enterprise Institute, author David Farabee (2005: xvi) argues that "the majority of rehabilitative programs have little or no lasting impact

on recidivism". Arguing that our "overemphasis on rehabilitation distracts prisons from performing their role of
protecting us" (p. 39), he calls for a shift to a hugely beefed
up deterrence system involving vastly reduced parole case-
loads and a widespread investment in satellite tracking
technologies:

> There is an extensive body of research literature that directly
> challenges the purported effectiveness of social programs on
> recidivism, and supports such common-sense approaches as
> increasing deterrence through closer monitoring. . . . To reduce
> recidivism, we must return to basic principles of behavior
> and do a better job of detecting crimes and swiftly applying
> sanctions. Change is possible without workbooks, videos, and
> group meetings.
>
> (pp. 76–7)

Echoing these views only a few months later, the American
Society of Criminology's *Criminology and Public Policy* published an essay by Douglas Marlowe (2006, p. 339), who
risked being branded "with the scarlet M (for Martinson)"
by arguing that "what works" in fact "never did":

> Because any negative finding could be interpreted as casting
> pallor on the concept of rehabilitation . . . investigators often
> feel compelled to declare victory at every turn. If their primary
> hypotheses are not confirmed, they can usually rely on post hoc
> correlations to elicit some evidence of treatment effects. And if
> that is insufficient, the failsafe position is to conclude that the
> intervention might not have been adequately implemented. . . .
> The literature is so rife with "noise" touting unproven inter-
> ventions that practitioners and policy makers have difficulty
> separating the wheat from the chaff.
>
> (p. 339)

To quote Cullen (2005), "How did this happen?" What happened to the victory of science over politics in the rehabilitation debate? Is the ghost of Martinson back to haunt criminology? We appear to have, again, entered a period of uncertainty about the relevance, value and effectiveness of offender rehabilitation. It is too early to tell for certain; but, if so, Cullen would not be the first president to stride on to a battlefield and proclaim "Mission accomplished" a bit prematurely.

FROM WHAT WORKS TO WHAT HELPS

Perhaps one way out of this pendular and seemingly unhelpful dispute between "nothing works" and "treatment works" is to abandon Martinson's two-word legacy altogether. As numerous observers have argued over the years, "What Works" is probably the "wrong question" (Lin, 2000) for the important issue of offender rehabilitation (see also Farrall, 2004; Mair, 2004; Maruna, 2001; Toch, 2002). Imagine, after all, that, rather than asking "What Works", Martinson had asked "What helps people go straight?" The difference in word choice is subtle enough. Presumably the two phrases mean essentially the same thing. Yet the difference in impact between the two questions is substantial (see Bottoms and McWilliams, 1979; McNeill, 2006; Raynor, 1985).

For one thing, it is easy to declare that "nothing works" when "works" implies some degree of predictable consistency (i.e. "reliably works every time"). Nothing "works" for every offender in every circumstance. Yet it would require an extremely unusual view of the social world for someone to declare "Nothing *helps* people go straight". Although many things might hinder this process (see Liebling and Maruna, 2005), surely some things can help it (Toch, 2002).

After all, despite all of the argy-bargy and back-and-forth about the effectiveness of treatment, hardly anyone (but the most extreme data-deniers among the hard Right) denies that most one-time offenders do "go straight" and desist from crime eventually. No one will ever measure the true frequency of this for certain, but criminal-career researchers estimate that something like 85 percent of repeat offenders desist from this activity by the age of 28 (Blumstein and Cohen, 1987). Unless this process is completely random, some things must be helpful in making this transition. To deny this is to deny everything most of us believe about the social world.

Another difference is that if a person is given help, and still does not go straight, the fault is usually not pointed at the helpers, but rather at the individual. The help might not have been "enough", and maybe the help provision needs improvement, but perhaps also the individual simply chose to reoffend despite the help. We rarely think of help "working" in the way we might evaluate a treatment or a cure. A computer is an enormous "help" to someone trying to write a book; few would deny that. Yet, if we asked "Do computers 'work' as book completers", the answer is clearly "No – and what an absurd question considering the fact that human book-writers have agency all of their own". No intervention – even one as profound as the provision of a computer – can take that away.

Consider also how we might go about addressing the two questions. With "what works", the implications are clear: We need random control trials, experimentation and meta-analyses across different programs. We need to measure the impact of different intervention dosages, in different contexts with different sorts of clients. Likewise, if the question is instead "What helps people go straight", all of the same studies are certainly useful. Yet one might also think to interview some ex-offenders – particularly those who have managed to go straight – and find out from them what helped and what did not. After all, if we wanted to know "What helps academics in their first year at a new job" or "What helps probation staff organize their time", the first thing we would do is to interview the persons involved and ask them. Additionally, we might also want to understand the process of desistance from crime more broadly – outside the very narrow context of "programs" – and learn from these wider experiences (see Lynch, 2006). As Farrall (1995) argues, "Most of the research suggests that desistance 'occurs' away from the criminal justice system. That is to say that very few people actually desist as a result of intervention on the part of the criminal justice system or its representatives" (p. 56). Indeed, arguably, the majority of criminal justice interventions appear more likely to impede the process of going straight by detaching individuals from their families, derailing career paths, and breeding hostility and defiance (see Liebling and Maruna, 2005, for a review of these damaging effects of imprisonment and other punishments).

It therefore makes considerable sense to develop models of rehabilitation on the basis of what is known about how reintegration works in the "natural" environment, outside the criminal justice system (see Lynch, 2006; Maruna, 2001). In fact, a growing movement in criminology argues that rehabilitation research should become "desistance-focused" in perspective (see especially Farrall, 2004; Farrant, 2006; Halsey, 2006; Harris, 2005; Lewis, 2005; Maguire and Raynor 2006; Maruna and Immarigeon, 2004; McCulloch, 2005; McNeill, 2003, 2006; Rex, 1999; Rumgay, 2004). McNeill (2006, p. 46) explains this movement thus: "Put simply, the implication is that offender management services need to think of themselves less as providers of correctional treatment (that belongs to the expert) and more as supporters of desistance processes (that belong to the desister)." Likewise, Farrall (2004) distinguishes "desistance-focused" perspectives from "offending-related" approaches on the basis that, whereas the latter concentrate on targeting offender deficits, the former seek to promote those strengths – e.g., strong social bonds, pro-social involvements and social capital – that appear to be related to successful efforts to go straight (see Laub and Sampson, 2001; Maruna, 2001).

WHAT DO OFFENDERS WANT?

In what follows, then, we shall address the question of "what helps people go straight" in the tradition of desistance-focused rehabilitation. Our argument has been developed over a number of years in discussions with colleagues and practitioners but, most importantly, our ideas have been shaped by listening to prisoners and probationers.[2] The participants in criminal justice interventions are an extraordinary untapped resource in the formulation of rehabilitation theory and policy, and our argument reflects what they have taught us in clinical and research settings over the years.

The first thing we need to know about the "offender perspective" is that – like everyone else apparently – even offenders hate "rehabilitation".[3] When you interview them, most prisoners and probationers will say they want to change their life and desist from crime, although they do not use that word, either, of course (see e.g., Burnett, 2004; Lin, 2000; Shover, 1996). They will happily talk about going straight, self-change, recovery or even redemption. Still, almost none will tell you that they need to be "rehabilitated", and they tend to be highly suspicious of structured rehabilitation programs – especially those with a psychological underpinning (as opposed to, for instance, job training) and those that emphasize risk. Drawing on her work with prisoners in Pennsylvania, M. Kay Harris (2005) summarizes this perspective perfectly:

Many people who are currently or were formerly in prison embrace the self-change, empowerment, and desistance perspective. They hold negative attitudes toward the concept of rehabilitation and correctional treatment programs. In general, the distaste for such programs is linked to a sense that these interventions involve things being "done to" or "prescribed for" passive recipients who are characterized as deficient, ineffectual, misguided, untrustworthy, possibly dangerous, and almost certain to get into trouble again. Although people who have been incarcerated often believe that some staff members or other outside parties and some types of programs can be helpful, their effectiveness stems from the potential they offer for empowering participants rather than trying to compel them to change. Most argue, "No one else can rehabilitate you. You rehabilitate yourself." If there is distaste for correctional treatment programs among people under correctional supervision, there is even stronger antipathy toward interventions tailored to actuarial risk assessments.

It is fascinating to think that prisoners and probationers are resistant to therapeutic treatments at the same time that the rest of us are going broke trying to afford to pay for counseling and therapy for ourselves and, increasingly, for our children (Hillman and Ventura, 1993). Where are the cries (so frequently heard in the debate about offering university-level education to prisoners) of unfairness? ("Why should *those people* get all the free counseling they want, when I have to pay thousands to keep my family and me in therapy?")

The answer, of course, is that "their" therapy is different from "our" therapy. As pointed out beautifully by Stanley Cohen (1985, p. 153), counseling for the affluent ("healthy neurotics or the worried well") involves a focus on "who you are": "feelings, insight, emotional growth, awareness and self-actualization". Contemporary adults are "only too willing to 'refer' themselves" to therapies like these that help us enjoy our lives, get an extra edge in the market-place, or gain insight into our daily struggles. As Cohen (1985, p. 154) writes, the motto of this voluntary self-help movement is "turn yourself in". This is a far cry from the rehabilitation that prisoners seem to resent so much. Here the focus is not on insight, but on behavior "sometimes accompanied by the rhetoric of cognition" (p. 154). The focus is on the tight restriction of one's actions, correction of "criminal thinking", resocialization, surveillance, and of course behavioral conditioning. Cohen writes: "This is a vision which will quite happily settle for sullen citizens, performing their duties, functioning with social skills, and not having any insights" (p. 151).

The rehabilitation client, after all, is not the real focus of the intervention, only his or her outward behavior. In fact, offender rehabilitation may be one of the only forms of treatment in existence that is explicitly intended for the benefit of others (the "community") rather than for the person undergoing the counseling itself. In fact, who cares what offenders want? Prisoners and probationers have proved themselves to be untrustworthy by virtue of their past actions, and surely the experts know what is needed more than this cast of characters.

As Michael Ignatieff argues in *The Needs of Strangers* (1984, p. 11), "There are few presumptions in human relations more dangerous than the idea that one knows what another human being needs better than they do themselves". If prisoners and probationers do not want the interventions we are providing for them, are these things any real help? Except for the most nightmarish among the imagined cures for criminality (e.g., the lobotomies, electric shocks and psychopharmaceutical treatments in works such as *A Clockwork Orange* and *One Flew Over the Cuckoo's Nest*), all forms of rehabilitation require the active acceptance and willing participation of intervention participants in order to work. Individuals can be forced to sit and listen, they can even be forced to participate in some talk therapy, but they cannot be forced to change. Efforts among "authorities" to force changes in an individual's personality will quite reasonably be met with resistance and defiance (see especially Duguid, 2000). Sutherland and Cressey (1978, p. 558) are right when they argue that all a prisoner has left is his sense of self or identity, and that "If it should be taken away from him, even in the name of rehabilitation or treatment, he will have lost everything".

Indeed, the drop-out/retention rates for most rehabilitative interventions are abysmal. The true level of engagement among even those who do attend regularly is often minimal, to say the least. In all of the meta-analytic number-crunching around the What Works debate, readers rarely get a glimpse of what actually goes on in rehabilitation programs themselves. Lin's important study *Reform in the Making* (2000), provides a rare peek inside this "black box" of program implementation:

> Six or seven of the men are sitting, heads in hands, staring at workbooks; the rest are sleeping, talking, or doodling. [The rehabilitation practitioner] reads a newspaper at her desk in front, looking up once in a while to restore order or answer a question when someone approaches her. Given the amount of sleeping and staring in the classroom, the occasions requiring her intervention are few.
>
> (p. 15)

Now, this is an unfair example and not at all meant to be representative of all forms of offender rehabilitation. Yet most practitioners will recognize classrooms such as this from their own experiences.

Our point is simply that, if participants themselves do

not engage with or commit themselves to an intervention, the "treatment" cannot really claim to be of much "help". Any rehabilitation option offered to prisoners and proba- tioners needs to make sense to clients themselves and be clearly relevant to the possibility of their living a better life. Other- wise there is little chance that individuals will gain anything useful from correctional practitioners' well-intentioned efforts. This view from the "offenders" themselves appears, to us, to be the most important issue neglected in the back-and- forth argument about whether rehabilitation "works".

THE ROAD AHEAD

In this book, we review and examine two models of offender rehabilitation in depth, the Risk–Need–Responsivity Model (Andrews and Bonta, 2003) and the Good Lives Model (Ward and Stewart, 2003). We have chosen these particular models because they are good examples of the two primary ways of working with offenders, the risk-management and the strength-based intervention approaches. We begin in Chapter 2 by outlining just what is meant by a "theory" of rehabilitation, what is required in a "good" theory and what such a theory can do. In Chapter 3 we outline in considerable detail the reigning paradigm in rehabilitation theory and practice. In the following chapter, we interrogate the assumptions and internal consistency of the model, and in Chapter 5 we present an alternative theoretical frame- work. This alternative theory is linked to quite different assumptions concerning the purpose of rehabilitation and the nature of criminality, which we spell out in Chapters 4 and 5. Out of a sense of balance, we then use Chapter 6 to explore the strengths and weaknesses of our own alternative model (although, biased as we are, we find more of the for- mer than of the latter). Finally, we conclude with a brief model for making peace between the reigning model and our alternative.

THE REIGNING PARADIGM IN REHABILITATION

The most common attitude toward offenders might be called the Risk Model. This perspective involves policies concerned with risk detection and management, where the focus is squarely on estimating the degree to which individuals constitute a menace to the community and then setting out to reduce or minimize their risk factors in the most cost-efficient manner. Individuals are viewed as bearers of risk, potential agents of harm or hazards. The rehabilitation approach most closely aligned to the risk-management perspective is the Risk–Need–Responsivity Model or what we shall refer to throughout as the RNR Model (see Andrews and Bonta, 2003). RNR is by far "the most coherent approach to treatment now available" (Gaes *et al.*, 1999, p. 363) and it is underpinned by an enormous body of empirical support (Andrews *et al.*, 1990; Andrews and Dowden, 2005; Cullen and Gendreau, 2000; Lipsey, 1992; MacKenzie, 2006).

The assumptions underlying the RNR model are well established in criminal justice agencies and non-government agencies throughout the Western world to the point where it can be regarded as the received or orthodox position concerning rehabilitation (Visher, 2006). In essence, RNR proposes that correctional interventions should be structured according to three core rehabilitation principles: risk, need and responsivity (Andrews and Bonta, 1998; Hollin, 1999). Perhaps the best-known rehabilitation assumption is that the most effective and ethical approach to the treatment of offenders is to target *dynamic risk factors* (i.e., criminogenic needs) that are causally related to criminal behavior (Andrews and Bonta, 1998; Gendreau and Andrews, 1990; Hanson,

2001; McGuire, 2000). This is termed the *need* principle. A second important guiding assumption is the *risk* principle, which specifies that the treatment of offenders ought to be organized according to the level of risk they pose to society. That is, the higher the level of the risk the greater the dosage or intensity of treatment should be. The third major assumption is the *responsivity* principle, which is primarily concerned with the problem of matching the delivery of correctional interventions to certain characteristics of participants (e.g., motivation, learning style, and ethnic identity). The intent of the responsivity principle is to ensure that therapeutic and other types of correctional intervention are implemented in a way that is likely to make sense to offenders and thus enable them to absorb the program content and make the changes necessary in their life to desist from further offending. We shall be describing the RNR model in greater detail in Chapters 3 and 4.

In recent years, clinicians and researchers have challenged certain aspects of the RNR model and argued that concentrating on reducing dynamic risk factors (criminogenic needs) is a *necessary* but *not sufficient* condition for effective correctional interventions (Ellerby, Bedard and Chartrand, 2000; Maruna, 2001; Ward and Stewart, 2003). One of the major concerns is the perceived narrowness of the RNR model and its failure to adopt a more constructive or positive approach to treatment. It has been argued that it is necessary to broaden the scope of correctional interventions to take into account the promotion of human goods (i.e., approach goals as well as avoidance goals): that is, experiences, activities or states of affairs that are strongly associated with the well-being and higher levels of personal satisfaction and social functioning (see Chapter 6).

Researchers, clinicians and correctional workers who are critical of the RNR model point to its inability to provide those involved with rehabilitation with sufficient tools to engage and work with offenders in the process of behavior change (see, e.g., Hannah-Moffat, 1999, 2005; Ward and Brown, 2003). What they mean by this claim is that a set of principles that are essentially oriented toward risk management and the allocation of scarce rehabilitation resources are unlikely to help deal with the complexities and demands of forensic practice.

In brief, those critical of the RNR model assert that:

(*a*) Motivating offenders by concentrating on eliminating or modifying their various dynamic risk factors is extremely difficult. One thing individuals want to know is how can they live a better life, what are the positive rewards in desisting from crime.

(*b*) The RNR model tends to neglect or under-emphasize the role of self-identity and personal agency (i.e., self-directed, intentional actions designed to achieve valued goals) in the change process. An important component of living an offense-free life appears to be viewing oneself as a different person with the capabilities and opportunities to achieve personally endorsed goals, yet this "whole person" perspective is downplayed in the risk framework.

(*c*) The RNR model appears to be associated with a rather restricted and passive view of human nature.

(*d*) The RNR model does not appreciate the relevance and crucial role of treatment alliance in the therapeutic process. Any type of enduring change depends on the capacity of the offender to trust his or her therapist enough to absorb the skills and "lessons" imparted in therapy. This means that so-called noncriminogenic needs such as personal distress and low self-esteem are essential clinical targets; failure to address them is likely to result in a weak therapeutic alliance (see Marshall, Fernandez *et al.*, 2003).

(*e*) The RNR model is fundamentally a psychometric model (i.e., derived from and in part based on data from reliable and valid measures of criminal behavior) and tends to be preoccupied with offenders' risk profiles (or traits) and downplays the relevance of contextual or ecological factors in offender rehabilitation. This ignores the fact that offenders, like all human beings, are embedded in various social and cultural systems that facilitate and constrain their behavior (Lynch, 2006).

(f) In variance with the responsivity principle, the RNR model is often implemented in practice in a "one size fits all" manner and fails adequately to consider the specific needs, values and issues of individual offenders. The fact that the RNR model is implemented in a large-scale, heavily manualized and prescriptive manner makes it difficult to accommodate the unique characteristics of offenders. In its most inappropriate form, the RNR model is translated into a psycho-educational format in which offenders are "taught" how to behave in a heavily didactic and counterproductive way (Green, 1995).

THE GOOD LIVES ALTERNATIVE

In recent years, in response to criticisms such as these, strengths-based or "restorative" approaches to working with offenders have been formulated as an alternative to the risk model of reintegration theory (see Burnett and Maruna, 2006; Maruna and LeBel, 2003; Raynor and Robinson, 2005; Ward and Gannon, 2006). Emerging out of the science of positive psychology (e.g., Seligman and Csikszentmihalyi, 2000), strengths-based approaches shift the focus away from criminogenic needs and other deficits and instead ask what the individual can contribute to his or her family, community and society. How can their life become useful and purposeful (see Ward and Brown, 2004)? The idea is not that prisoners and probationers do not have any needs that must be met or pose any particular risks; only, the problem with these preoccupations and with the practices that they produce is that ". . . they tend to accentuate precisely those aspects of an offender's history, behaviour and attitudes which intervention aims to diminish" (McNeill, 2003, pp. 155–6). By contrast, strengths-based or "desistance-focused" approaches allow for the reconstruction of a new generative identity, instead of unwittingly reinforcing the passivity and fatalism of the old identity (Bazemore, 2004).

The most systematically developed theory in the strengths-based domain is probably Ward and colleagues' "Good Lives Model" (see Ward and Brown, 2004; Ward and Gannon, 2006; Ward and Stewart, 2003). The Good Lives Model (or GLM) begins from the assumption that offenders are essentially human beings with similar needs and aspirations to nonoffending members of the community. In his important review, Duguid (2000, p. 18) describes this as treating prisoners as "subjects rather than objects": "appreciate their complexity, treat them with respect, and demand reciprocity". The GLM is based around two core therapeutic goals: to promote human goods and to reduce risk. According to Ward and his colleagues, a focus on the promotion of specific goods or goals in the treatment of offenders is likely automatically to eliminate (or reduce) commonly targeted dynamic risk factors (or criminogenic needs). By contrast, they argue that focusing *only* on the reduction of risk factors is unlikely to promote the full range of specific goods and goals necessary for longer-term desistence from offending.

Strength-based approaches such as the *Good Lives Model* (GLM) of offender rehabilitation: (*a*) focus on the utilization of an individual offender's primary goods or values in the design of intervention programs and (*b*) aim to equip him with the capabilities necessary to implement a better life plan founded on these values. The GLM is an approach based on the pursuit of a better life, ways of living that are constructed around core values, and concrete means of realizing their goals in certain environments (Ward and Stewart,

2003). This argument will be systematically developed over the following chapters.

PROCEEDING WITH ALL DUE APPREHENSION

We recognize that the topic of rehabilitation is dangerous terrain and we tread here with much trepidation. Many a criminologist has been burned in the "what works" debates, and most have learned to avoid the rehabilitation argument at all costs out of self-preservation. Indeed, no other debate in criminology (with the possible exception of gun control) is as explicitly and obviously political, and yet no other debate features half as many claims (on all sides!) to being the voice of objective, call-'em-like-I-see-'em "Science" with a capital S. For a "cuddly" subject, the intellectual battles around rehabilitation have been fierce, gloves-off affairs leaving many bruised egos and worse (!) along the way. After all, unlike some other areas of criminological science, there is money to be made in rehabilitation – lots of it in some cases. With such high stakes, there is a temptation to attack and discredit any potential critics or competitors in the intellectual arena for fear of loss of one's market share. Indeed, RNR proponents sometimes claim that critics of their theory are engaging in "knowledge destruction" (with a nod to Gottfredson, 1979).

In this framework, "destructive" critics focus on what does not work in rehabilitation, but do not offer any practical alternatives. As such, we hope it will be clear in what follows that – although we are critical of the RNR theory – we are not "knowledge destructors" who simply enjoy the role of the contrarian. In what follows, in addition to interrogating the RNR model, we also put our own necks on the line by spelling out in some detail an alternative, although complementary, framework for rehabilitative work. In addition, we seek to preserve the many strengths of the RNR model in our own framework.

No rehabilitation theory can survive without the influx of new ideas or perspectives – especially the input of those persons participating in the interventions themselves. We offer this book, therefore, in the spirit of "knowledge construction" in hopes of improving existing service delivery and helping people live a good life. Academic simpletons we very well may be, but perhaps a bit of simplicity (or transparency?) is exactly what is needed to help save rehabilitation from becoming a dirty word.

2

WHAT IS A REHABILITATION THEORY?

The vast majority of academic work in rehabilitation is empirical in nature. The literature is replete with quasi-experimental evaluations and meta-analyses of these results, and numerous voices from all sides of the rehabilitation debate (see, e.g., Farabee, 2005) have argued forcefully that what is needed in rehabilitation is more "true" experiments. Yet all of this empirical work may be putting the cart before the horse. Lynch (2006, p. 408) argues that the study of reentry or rehabilitation is arguably "not ready for experiments" and that "going out of one's way to conduct experiments and quasi-experiments would be a very wasteful way of producing knowledge about what encourages success-ful reentry".[1] In short, for experiments to be useful, we need a clear theory of how "what works" is actually supposed to function (see Chen, 1990; Pawson and Tilley, 1997). At the very minimum, Lynch argues, we should be able to differentiate between the experiences of the experimental group and of the control group!

This sounds fairly obvious, yet for much of its history the practice of rehabilitation has taken place within a theoretical vacuum, with no clear explanation for how the process is supposed to work (see Simon, 1993). In short, rehabilitation research frequently asks "what works" but too often neglects the issue of "*how it works*" (see Lin, 2000; Palmer, 1994). The impact of this lack of clear theory has been substantial. First, it has meant that the rehabilitation work that goes on inside and outside prisons today is too haphazard and ill-planned (see Cohen, 1985; Crow, 2001; Lynch, 2006; Morgan and Owers, 2001; Maguire and Raynor, 2006; Re-entry Policy Council, 2005). Referring to the typical work of probation and parole departments, Maloney, Bazemore and Hudson (2001, p. 24) quip: "If there is an intervention theory in use, it is generally based on the rather bizarre assumption that surveillance and some guidance can steer the offender straight." Second, even those interventions that are explicitly modeled on evidenced-based correctional models (i.e. what works) frequently fail because of the program's inability to implement the intervention as designed (see Lin, 2000; Lewis *et al.*, 2003). The sheer frequency of "implementation" failures – described as "the bane of effective correctional intervention" (Rhine, Mawhorr and Parks, 2006) – surely reflects upon a lack of clarity in the rehabilitation models being delivered.

Indeed, much of the blame for this lack of theoretical development, of course, lies with academic criminology. It is our job, after all, to develop and test theories of criminal processes. Yet, as Cullen (2002, p. 283) writes, "Although criminology is rich in contemporary theories of crime, true theories of correctional intervention are in short supply. One searches in vain in mainstream criminology journals and textbooks for new systematic theories of intervention."

Too often, rehabilitation is spoken about by criminologists in a sort of code language: Offenders should receive "appropriate treatment" that is "clinically relevant" and "psychologically informed". Yet often we are not told what this actually means in enough detail to judge the practices.

Robert Martinson (1976), in one of his more colorful attacks on the rehabilitative ideal, laid out this challenge to treatment supporters in no uncertain terms:

> But what specifically is the method? Probation-like placement? Small caseloads? Unadulterated love? What is it? What is the actual process that takes place by which "recidivism" is reduced? If [one of the rehabilitation supporters] knew which "element" or "dimension" of [the treatment] was having whatever effect he thinks he has found, he surely would not keep it such a secret. He would patent it, sell it around the country to our administrators, be given the Congressional Medal of Honor, and retire to the Bahamas, an honored and wealthy man. [The academic rehabilitation proponent] can talk for twenty pages in the special language we all know so well, but he cannot bring himself to say in plain English to my neighbors, who are waiting with bated breath, just what this process is.

Although characteristically overstated, Martinson's point is valid. Every criminologist knows what rehabilitation is, but few of us have actually described how it is supposed to work. Like others, Cullen (2002) blames this lack of theoretical innovation on the legacy of the "nothing works" challenge to the practice of rehabilitation. "Developing theories of effective intervention seemed ill advised if there was, in essence, no 'treatment effect' to be explained" (p. 283).

WHAT IS THEORY?

This chapter will describe those features required to develop a working theory of rehabilitation: What is a good rehabilitation theory and what does it do? In brief, a theory is a description of an unobserved aspect of the world and may consist of a collection of interrelated laws or a systematic set of ideas (Kukla, 2001). We acknowledge that this is a rather loose definition of "theory" but are keen to be as inclusive as possible in our consideration of explanatory and interpretative theories. There are a number of philosophies of science evident in the social, behavioral and natural sciences, each possessing its own assumptions concerning what constitutes an adequate explanation, a good theory, the nature of causality, and how best to characterize truth (Newton-Smith, 2002). The available (and contested!) philosophies of science include empiricism, instrumentalism, logical positivism, social constructionism, various forms of post-positivism, realism and conventionalism.

In a relatively small book such as this one, it is impractical to sift through all the possibilities and to argue rigorously for our guiding metaphysical, epistemological and normative commitments. However, it is necessary to outline our basic meta-theoretical assumptions in enough detail to allow readers to follow our overall argument and style of analysis. To lay our cards on the table, therefore, we adopt a critical realist view of science in this book (Hooker, 1987; Psillos, 1999). According to scientific realism, individuals construct theories of their social and physical world in order to enhance their understanding of the way it works and to solve theoretical and practical problems. The satisfactory solution of such problems requires researchers to depict accurately the mechanisms and structures lying beneath the surface of life that, through their generative activity, create the rich array of phenomena evident in the world. It is important to note that social rules and discursive practice can be regarded as "mechanisms" alongside typical causal factors such as intimacy deficits and impulsivity. From a critical realist perspective, the world is viewed as multifaceted and constituted by complex systems of various kinds. Thus, any explanatory efforts will need to proceed on different levels and seek to develop multiple lines of analysis. The fact that individuals' interests determine what counts as (valuable) knowledge means that human values (as evident in needs and interests) guide the application of scientific knowledge and methods to the everyday world. If these representations are accurate (or useful!), people's interests will be promoted and needs met, but failure to get it right may result in impaired problem-solving and subsequent unhappiness and dissatisfaction. It is pertinent to note that from a critical realist view of science there is merit in the postmodern claim that the "world is constructed" but only in the sense that scientific knowledge underpins actions that modify the world, the consequences of which may prove to be beneficial or harmful. Ideas shape the contours of our everyday lives through their ability to guide action.

We believe that good theories provide researchers with cognitive maps of the way the world works and thus are a useful intellectual resource for the construction and implementation of technologies and ways of living. Furthermore, such tools and practical knowledge can help people control aspects of their life and environment and to solve pressing social and personal problems such as crime, pollution and disease. The point of the term "critical realism" is openly to admit the provisional nature of our understanding of the social and physical world; our version of realism, therefore, is a rather modest one (see Kitcher, 2001). We accept that even our best theories may only be partially true and that it is possible that for any given scientific problem there could be more than one way of solving it. Scientific theories and research problems always reflect human values and interests; and, given that these can legitimately vary, the concerns of different groups often may result in the formulation of diverse problems and therefore solutions.

In brief, scientific theories of human behavior have two primary aims: explanation of important phenomena, and the prediction and control of the relevant aspects of such phenomena, for example, sexual offending or disease (e.g. see Ward, Polaschek and Beech, 2006). Therefore, a theory should be able to provide an account of why certain things happen the way they do and why they have the features they do. Theories are used both to explain and to predict phenomena. Explanation is basically the application of a theory in order to help understand certain phenomena and is backward-looking (i.e. helps understand why a particular outcome happened). By contrast, prediction is forward-looking and is concerned with the forecasting of outcomes within a person, group, institution or physical system.

FEATURES OF A GOOD REHABILITATION THEORY

In order to be able adequately to describe and evaluate the Risk–Need–Responsivity (RNR) Model and the Good Lives Model (GLM) it is first necessary to identify the essential features of a rehabilitation theory. We argue that a good theory of offender rehabilitation should specify the aims of therapy, provide a justification of these aims in terms of its core assumptions about etiology and the values underpinning the approach, identify clinical targets, and outline how treatment should proceed in the light of these assumptions and goals (Ward and Marshall, 2004).

Somewhat surprisingly, we have found that the nature of rehabilitation tends to be taken for granted in the correctional field and very little has been said about what actually constitutes a *rehabilitation theory* as opposed to a type of therapy (e.g. cognitive-behaviorism or psychodynamic) or a broad field of psychological thought (e.g. cognitive or humanistic psychology). Moreover, when practitioners or researchers do refer to rehabilitation theory, this term is often used interchangeably with either normative theories (e.g. policy debates about why we should offer rehabilitation at all) or etiological theories (e.g. why people commit crime) or treatment theories (e.g. how best to implement treatment practices).

This unfortunate conflation of distinct types of theory can lead, at best, to confusion about how to proceed when working therapeutically with prisoners and probationers and, at worst, to a failure to provide correctional workers with a comprehensive framework for dealing with the complexities of correctional practice. Typically, there is little attention given to policy or etiological theories, and most often what is presented to rehabilitation practitioners is manual-based programs that prescribe in great detail "how-to" techniques for the implementation of a treatment program. This is a far cry from a rehabilitation theory. In contrast to rehabilitation theories, treatment theories involve psychological principles and concrete strategies applied to work in clinical settings intended to change the behavior of individuals. They are in effect local theories of change and specify how to effect reductions in offense-related problems using certain types of technique.

A complete "rehabilitation theory" is broader in nature and refers to the overarching aims, values, principles, justifications and etiological assumptions that are used to guide interventions and help therapists translate these rather abstract principles into practice. Rehabilitation theory, therefore, is essentially a *hybrid* theory comprised of values, core principles, etiological assumptions and practice guidelines. In effect, it contains elements of normative, etiological and practice/treatment theories within it while being somewhat broader than just the sum of these parts. It contains multiple levels and enables correctional workers to intervene in diverse but coherent ways. Without a rehabilitation theory, practitioners and clients will be unaware of the broad aims of an intervention and their relationship to the causes of offending.

We propose that there are *three* (see Figure 2.1) levels or components to rehabilitation theories: (A) a set of general principles and assumptions that specify the values and views that underlie rehabilitation practice and the kind of overall aims for which clinicians should be striving; (B) etiological assumptions that serve to explain offending and identify its functions, at least in a general sense; and (C) the intervention implications of both A and B. It is useful to think of the three levels as hierarchically structured and each necessary for the level below it. To illustrate in backward order: to be able to set clear treatment targets and to deal with the demands of correctional practice (component C), it is necessary to hold some causal assumptions (component B). In turn, the type of causal assumptions endorsed depends on the overarching assumptions about human nature and

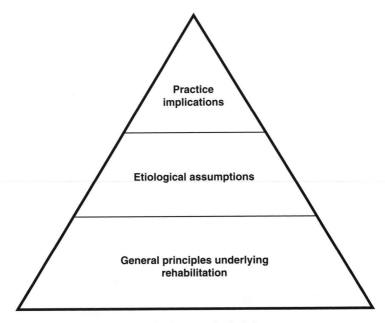

Figure 2.1 Components of a theory of rehabilitation

orientations toward intervention held by the workers and institutions involved (component A). Each level is discussed in greater detail below.

GENERAL PRINCIPLES AND ASSUMPTIONS

Every rehabilitation theory has a number of general metaphysical, epistemological, ethical and normative principles concerning the purpose of and nature of the key actors associated with rehabilitation underlying its practical suggestions. In our experience, these are often tacit and require teasing out (see Chapters 4 and 6).

Metaphysical assumptions concern the nature of the entities involved in the rehabilitation process and delineate their core features and processes. As rehabilitation is an inescapably human enterprise – with humans helping other humans – the core metaphysical concern is with human nature in general. Are human beings born naturally selfish as in a Hobbesian model or are we naturally social beings inclined to work together as in Rousseau's model? Where does the theory sit in terms of the crucial nature-versus-nurture issue and the question of human plasticity? Can people change their core selves or is personality, especially for those deemed to be criminal or disordered, largely immutable? Other metaphysical questions involve the nature of constructs such as "criminals", "crime", "risk" and "treatment"/"help". Are some individuals (e.g. "psychopaths") permanently incapable of core human emotions such as empathy or love? Is crime to be understood as a social/legal construction, a moral violation, or an infringement on the human rights of others? Is risk to be understood as discrete or dynamic? Does risk reside within the person or in the situation? Finally, in the rehabilitation process, who *does* the rehabilitating? Is a medical model presumed whereby practitioners rehabilitate passive clients or is a process of self-help presumed? All of these assumptions – even when they are not made explicitly in theoretical statements or treatment manuals – play a crucial role in shaping rehabilitation practices.

The basic *epistemological* assumptions really spell out what constitutes knowledge and how research that informs practice should be undergone. It will include recommendations about research designs, analytic strategies, and what kind of evidence is admissible when deciding on best practice. In addition, the core epistemological assumptions contained in a rehabilitation theory should inform researchers and practitioners about what knowledge in an abstract sense consists of and what threshold is required when making decisions (e.g. risk assessment, probation reports, etc.). The issue of threshold refers to cutoff points or boundaries that inform decision-makers when a critical value has been reached. Just where the cutoff point is depends on the consequences of having false positives or false negatives (e.g. falsely asserting that someone is dangerous versus falsely asserting that someone is not). An example of what we mean by core epistemological assumptions is evident in the ongoing debate concerning the merits of qualitative versus quantitatively derived data. In this dispute, constructivist approaches to knowledge privilege personal or lived experience while positivist, empiricist theories favor more objective data yielded by psychometrically robust measures.

Ethical values are a particularly important set of resources as they represent foundational or core standards used to construct ways of living and behaving. They bestow a sense of meaning, significance and purpose on human lives and are at the heart of the rehabilitation process. A value judgment asserts that specific types of quality, which are evaluated as positive or negative, characterize aspects of the world or people (Kekes, 1993; Rescher, 1993). In brief, value judgments reveal what individuals consider to be of worth and beneficial to themselves or others. *Cognitive values* are features of beliefs or theories and their formation that indicate their likely truth (e.g., scope, explanatory depth, consistency). *Moral values* are usefully defined as humanly caused benefits that human beings provide to others, and they can be described as right or wrong, good or bad (Kekes, 1993). *Prudential values* are humanly caused benefits that people secure for themselves or are naturally occurring benefits received or derived from nonhuman sources resulting in enhanced well-being (Griffin, 1996; Kekes, 1993). Core prudential values (or human goods) are benefits that meet individual self-interests (Ward and Stewart, 2003).

Values play a significant role in rehabilitation theories as they serve to identify therapeutic goals and to constrain rehabilitative attempts (e.g. we should not subject individuals to empirically unsupported interventions or expose them to unnecessarily stressful situations – prisoners and probationers should be respected as moral agents not treated as means to the ends of researchers or correctional workers). In addition, the relative weightings of individuals' interests relative to those of the community will be stated and function to constrain therapeutic and bureaucratic decision-making – although we must reiterate our earlier point that these core values are implicit in what researchers say or do, and are often not articulated in specific discourses or practice guidelines.

Finally, *normative principles* regarding the justifications for intervening in the first place also underlie all rehabilitative theories. What gives one person/group the right to intervene in another's life? Under what circumstances is such intervention justified and under what conditions is it justifiable not to offer such an intervention? The core issues here (reviewed above in Chapter 1) include the question of coercion and the interplay between rehabilitation and punishment, needs and deserts (see Bottoms and McWilliams, 1979; McNeill, 2006).

ETIOLOGICAL ASSUMPTIONS

Etiological assumptions help correctional workers and therapists to understand what treatment goals are important and why. The etiological component of a rehabilitation theory is clearly linked to level A above and will incorporate those basic assumptions and principles in any causal claims. The etiological component bridges the gap between the core assumptions (component A) and practice guidelines (component C). If correctional work is to be effective, all of those involved (practitioners and clients) need a firm understanding of the origins and triggers of offending behaviors. However, these theories of etiology themselves are premised on core assumptions about human nature and ethical/ normative principles regarding social justice, morality and human diversity. In other words, scientific explanations track interests and values: researchers with different interests are likely to pursue quite different approaches to criminological knowledge development.

Rehabilitation theories should not be confused with etiological theories of a general type (e.g. general theories of crime) or of particular types of offense (e.g. sexual offenses). The major function of rehabilitation theories is to provide a comprehensive guide to clinicians when working with offenders. The etiological component of such theories is therefore quite general in scope. It only serves to sketch out the causal factors that might increase the likelihood of criminal actions and to depict their relationships with each other. In a sense it provides an *overview* of the kinds of factor that are likely to cause crimes and on its own does not constitute a complete explanation. In effect, because rehabilitation theories are hybrid theories containing elements of different types of theory, they can not be expected to provide the same kind of value that the more specific, predictive theories do in their own particular domains. In a sense, they hover above the more specific theories and draw from them core assumptions and factors. Ultimately the content-rich or domain-specific theories (e.g. theories of crime) feed into or provide the more abstract "rehabilitation" with theory content. This should be an ongoing explicit and critical process. That is, policy-makers, researchers and practitioners should deliberately evaluate their best rehabilitation theories in light of new criminological research and either adjust the theory or reject it for a better alternative as new research emerges.

INTERVENTION IMPLICATIONS

Finally, the third component of a good rehabilitation theory is the implications for intervention: the "how to" guide for effective interventions. Whereas the first two aspects of rehabilitation theory are often only implicit or implied, this level is the most overt. Every rehabilitation theory needs to specify the most suitable style of treatment (e.g. skills-based, structured, etc.), inform therapists about the appropriate attitudes to take toward offenders, address the issue of motivation, and clarify the role and nature of the therapeutic relationship. Intervention implications include the recommended screening mechanisms for the matching of the individual participant with intervention type, the criteria on which to base decisions about "dosage" (this is a terrible term usually used to mean hours of involvement) and "intensity" (e.g. one-on-one attention versus group-based work) of the intervention.

Beyond this, however, it is incumbent on a theory to explain how the intervention itself is supposed to work. That is, what are the proposed change mechanisms at work in the intervention process? Oddly, this core aspect of rehabilitation theory is often missing from discussions of rehabilitation. Overburdened by discussions of assessment, classification and matching, rehabilitation theories tend to be rather silent in regard to the question of just what is to be done once an accurate risk–needs assessment is made. To say that projects work by "targeting" these factors and ignoring others is, of course, not enough. What is needed is an explanation of the targeting itself and its role in change processes (see Prochaska and DiClemente, 1982).

Importantly, the kind of guidance given to therapists will vary according to the core assumptions and etiological elements described earlier (see Figure 2.1). The three components are conceptually linked in that the overriding aims of rehabilitation should be consistent with the demonstrated causes of crime and the types of treatment intervention ought to follow from both etiological assumptions and core value commitments. Although theories of therapy assume the relevance and truthfulness of some etiological theories, they do not aim to explain why individuals commit offenses but instead concentrate on informing clinicians how to effect behavioral changes in individuals. In other words, there are various types of theory associated with criminality: rehabilitation theories, etiological theories, policy/normative theories and treatment theories.

EVALUATION OF REHABILITATION THEORIES

It remains to consider how best to evaluate rehabilitation theories. This is not straightforward as they are not scientific theories in any obvious sense, even though they do contain etiological assumptions that are explanatory. In other words, evaluating rehabilitation theories is a lot more difficult than asking "what works" (and that itself is no easy question!) and testing competing models of one theory against one another in an experimental or quasi-experimental design. Indeed, typically more than one theory is able to account for the empirical evidence, and our epistemological and normative assumptions are likely to influence the interpretation of these results in any case. As such, in view of the hybrid nature of rehabilitation theories and the mixture of ethical, scientific and practice-theoretical elements they contain, we suggest that the epistemic values listed below can be employed critically to ascertain their overall value (see also Andrews and Bonta, 2003; Newton-Smith, 2002; Ward, Polaschek and Beech, 2006).

Philosophers have suggested that a number of *epistemic or cognitive* values (i.e. theory appraisal criteria) are equally important for making comparisons between competing theoretical explanations (Hooker, 1987; Newton-Smith, 2002): empirical adequacy (whether the theory can account for existing findings), internal coherence (whether a theory contains contradictions or logical gaps), external consistency (whether the theory in question is consistent with other background theories that are currently accepted), unifying power (whether a theory can unify aspects of a domain of research that were previously viewed as separate), fertility (whether a theory can lead to new predictions and open up new avenues of inquiry or practice), simplicity (whether a theory makes the fewest special assumptions) and explanatory depth (whether the theory can describe deep underlying mechanisms and processes).

Because rehabilitation theories are richly textured and contain multiple internal theories, evaluation on all of these levels involves a twofold evaluation strategy. First, each of the three components of the theory should be critically examined to ascertain whether or not there are problems of coherence, scope and so forth. This is possible because sometimes important values are missing (i.e. ones endorsed by the community or a relevant professional group) or dubious assumptions made about offenders. Furthermore, the evidential basis of the various etiological claims ought to be examined and the various methods used to collect data should be critically appraised.

Second, an overall judgment can be made of the rehabilitation theory's value, taking into account its strengths and weaknesses relative to its rivals and also itself (i.e., with respect to the theory's overall balance of strengths and weaknesses). It is often the case that competing theories will exhibit some of the epistemic values described above and fail to evidence others. For example, a theory may be elegant but lack explanatory depth while another may be unduly complex but account for the deep structure of a domain in a more satisfactory way. Unfortunately there is really no substitute for judgment, so in such cases researchers will simply need to weigh up the strengths and weaknesses of competing theories and decide which to favor. Of course, sometimes the most rational decision is to pursue more than one theory and research program at the same time – a "let a thousand flowers bloom" strategy. Hopefully, in such cases, time (and more research!) will tell which of the rival theories is the best bet. The "best" theory (i.e. most useful, coherent and approximate to the "truth") is able to account for the agreed-upon facts of offending (by virtue of its etiological assumptions), has sufficient unifying power to incorporate important facets of rehabilitation (such as motivation, therapeutic alliance, skills acquisition, etc.), is relatively simple, has sufficient explanatory depth to clarify whether certain causal factors should be targeted in treatment, is both internally and externally consistent, and results in innovative and effective therapy.

CONCLUSIONS

We have argued that rehabilitation theories are vital resources for intervention staff, administrators, policy-makers, and most especially for the clients involved in rehabilitation work. Rehabilitation theories have a different structure from intervention theories, one that is frequently blurred by correctional workers and researchers. They provide a comprehensive guide for navigating one's way through the reintegration process, as opposed to simply an intervention plan for a particular type of problem. We have presented a novel organization for rehabilitation theories, proposing that they have a three-tier structure, with each level depending on the next: basic assumptions (metaphysical, epistemological and value), etiological assumptions, and practice strategies. A useful analogy for rehabilitation theories is that they function like topological maps, providing a broad overview of a city or country's key features and their interrelationships. Without such a map, it is easy to get confused and lost (and many treatment programs and participants do!). To this end we have listed a number of key theory-appraisal criteria and an accompanying strategy for evaluating the two rehabilitation theories described in this book.

3

THE RISK–NEED–RESPONSIVITY MODEL OF OFFENDER REHABILITATION

The Risk–Need–Responsivity (RNR) Model first emerged out of Canada in the 1980s, during the heyday of the "nothing works" pessimism around rehabilitation. In the wonderful phrase of Canadian Stephen Duguid (2000), its emergence was like "a cold wind from the North" sweeping across North America and later to Europe and beyond. In this chapter and the next we shall describe the RNR Model in depth and then systematically evaluate it utilizing the epistemic (epistemological) criteria outlined in the previous chapter. However, it is first necessary to discuss briefly the concepts of risk, need and responsivity, since any evaluation of the RNR Model hinges on how these concepts are interpreted.

THE CONCEPT OF RISK

Risk refers to the possibility of harmful consequences occurring (Douglas, 1992). Risk has two major components: the existence of potentially harmful agents (people, animals, diseases, toxins, situations, etc.) and the possibility that the hazards associated with the agents in question will actually occur (Denny, 2005). Risk assessment is an indeterminate (uncertain) process and involves the application of procedures for ascertaining the probability of a harmful event occurring within a specified time period. It involves judgments by individuals about the nature of the harm involved and the likelihood of a harmful event actually happening (Denny, 2005).

The concept of risk is clearly value-based (Kekes, 1989) and can be approached from a variety of theoretical perspectives. These range from positivist approaches that view risk factors as independent variables to cultural accounts where risk is hypothesized to be socially and politically constructed by different groups and not able to be adequately measured (Beck, 1992; Brown, 2000; Douglas, 1985; Young, 1999). In an important analysis of risk in what he calls the "risk society", Beck (1992, p. 42) asserts that "Basically one is no longer concerned with attaining something 'good' but rather preventing the worst". The idea is that individuals and institutions are increasingly concerned with avoiding a variety of dangers and holding others accountable when harm is experienced.

In the criminal justice process, risk assessment is the process of determining an individual's potential for harmful behavior toward himself or herself or others (see Feeley and Simon, 1992). The account of risk assumed by proponents of RNR and the majority of correctional workers appears to be an individualist or psychometric one. It is assumed that risk factors exist independently in the world rather than simply reflecting individuals' subjective concerns and once quantified can be used to estimate accurately the chances of adverse events (predominantly reoffending) taking place. Thus, a risk factor is a variable that increases the chances that an individual will behave in a harmful manner (see Blackburn, 2000). This influence may change over a person's life, and may vary across people, situations and developmental pathways (McGuire, 2000; Mrazek and Haggerty, 1994).

Risk factors may fall within four broad domains: (1) dispositional factors such as psychopathic or antisocial personality characteristics, cognitive variables, and demographic data; (2) historical factors such as adverse developmental history, prior history of crime and violence, prior hospitalization, and poor treatment compliance; (3) contextual antecedents to violence such as criminogenic needs (risk factors of criminal behavior), deviant social networks, and lack of positive social supports; and (4) clinical factors such as psychological disorders, poor level of functioning, and substance abuse (Andrews and Bonta, 1998; Blackburn, 2000; Hollin, 1999; McGuire, 2000). Risk factors are also commonly conceptualized as *static or dynamic* risk factors. Static factors are those risk variables that cannot change such as previous offense history, lack of long-term relationships, and general criminality. *Stable dynamic* risk factors are those risk variables that tend to be stable over time but are amenable to change; that is, sexual interests/sexual self-regulation, pro-offending attitudes, socio-affective functioning, and general self-regulation. *Acute dynamic* risk factors are those factors that change and fluctuate from one situation to another, such as mood state and substance abuse which can signal the onset of offending.

THE CONCEPT OF NEED

The concept of "need" is related to "risk" in the sense that individuals whose needs are not met might be said to be at risk of a harm of some sort; indeed, an unmet need is in some ways a harm in itself. After all, to have a need typically indicates a lack or deficiency of some kind, in particular a lack of a significant good (Braybrooke, 1987; Thomson, 1987). Maslow (1970) famously outlined a hierarchy of human needs with four levels of "deficiency needs" involving, in order: physiological needs, safety needs, love/belonging, and status/esteem needs. Maslow argued that all of these deficiency needs must be met for healthy growth and development, and that behavior is shaped in many ways by pursuit of fulfilling these needs. When these deficiency needs are met, Maslow theorized, humans can pursue a further level of "being needs" involving self-actualization and self-transcendence. This higher level of need involves peak experiences, creative pursuits, becoming "all that you can be" (as television commercials for the US Army promise).

More recently, Deci and Ryan (2000) have developed a self-determination theory of needs that is particularly useful for thinking about needs in the correctional context. Self-determination theory states that human beings are inherently active, self-directed organisms who are naturally predisposed to seek autonomy, relatedness and competence. Although this is a recent theoretical formulation, the idea that "agency" and "communion" (Bakan, 1966) are primary motivations for behavior can be traced back at least to the pre-Socratic philosopher Empedocles. Dan McAdams and his colleagues (1996, p. 340) write "That human lives are animated by two broad and contrasting tendencies resembling Bakan's concepts of agency and communion is an idea that is at least 2,000 years old". Agency and communion themes (i.e. work and love) were also central to Freud's theory of adult development and have been a central feature of almost every scientific effort to quantify significant aspects of interpersonal behavior for at least the last forty-five years (see the review in Wiggins, 1991). Deci and Ryan (2000, p. 229), however, go further than these previous understandings by defining autonomy and relatedness as needs or "innate psychological nutriments that are essential for ongoing psychological growth, integrity, and well-being".

Human needs involve the conditions essential for psychological well-being and fulfillment, and individuals can only flourish if they are met. Deci and Ryan suggest the failure to meet the three basic needs for autonomy, relatedness and competence will inevitably cause psychological distress and will likely result in the acquisition of maladaptive defenses. In other words, thwarted basic needs result in stunted lives, psychological problems and social maladjustment. Under these circumstances individuals acquire *substitute needs* that give them at least some degree of relatedness, competence and autonomy. However, the goals associated with these proxy needs are likely to result in a poorly integrated self, ultimately frustrating and unsatisfying relationships, self-esteem disturbances, and a sense of personal helplessness (for research evidence, see Deci and Ryan, 2000). Deci and Ryan argue that in order to experience a sense of enduring well-being all three needs have to be fulfilled; social conditions that pit one need against the other are likely to result in defensive motives and the development of substitute needs. The outcome of this forced accommodation is reduced levels of well-being.

Proponents of the RNR model of rehabilitation define needs more explicitly as personal deficits, but argue that only certain of these deficits or shortcomings are related to offending. They make this distinction explicit in their differentiation between two types of need: "criminogenic needs" and "noncriminogenic needs". Criminogenic needs include pro-offending attitudes, aspects of antisocial personality (e.g. impulsiveness), poor problem-solving abilities, substance-abuse problems, high hostility and anger, and criminal associates (Andrews and Bonta, 2003). These are contrasted with noncriminogenic needs, which, according to the RNR model, are aspects of the individual or his or her circumstances that if changed may not have a direct impact on recidivism rates. Examples of noncriminogenic needs are clinical phenomena such as low self-esteem (see Baumeister, 1999) and mental health problems such as depression or unresolved grief (but see De Coster and Heimer, 2001). In this framework, it is difficult to distinguish between a "criminogenic need" and a "risk factor" as both denote an empirically determined correlate of criminal offending.

THE CONCEPT OF RESPONSIVITY

Finally, the concept of responsivity is concerned with how an individual interacts with the treatment environment, covering a range of factors and situations. As such, responsivity (partly) involves an individual's motivation to engage in therapy and to commit to change (Miller and Rollnick, 2002; Prochaska and DiClemente, 1998). Responsivity is usually understood in the rehabilitation literature as primarily concerned with therapist and therapy features and is, therefore, essentially concerned with adjusting treatment delivery in a way that maximizes change (e.g. see Horvath and Luborsky, 1993).

The responsivity principle states that correctional programs should be matched to the offender's learning style, level of motivation, and personal and interpersonal circumstances. The principle of responsivity is based on the selection of interventions that are capable of making the desired changes and that match the offender's learning style (Andrews *et al.*, 1990). Responsivity may be usefully partitioned into two related ideas of specific and general responsivity. *Specific responsivity* refers to the individual characteristics of offenders which will make them more or less likely to engage with treatment. These characteristics typically include such factors as language skills, interpersonal skills, motivation and anxiety. For example, an unmotivated offender may be less likely to benefit from treatment. *General responsivity* describes the role of treatment-level issues in the match between treatment modality and offenders' learning styles (Andrews and Bonta, 2003).

Andrews (2001) further divides responsivity into internal and external responsivity. Attention to *internal responsivity* factors requires therapists to match the content and pace of sessions to specific client attributes such as personality and cognitive maturity. On the other hand, *external responsivity* refers to a range of general and specific issues, such as the use of active and participatory methods and consideration of the individual's life circumstances, culture, etc. Additionally, external responsivity can be divided further into staff and setting characteristics (Serin and Kennedy, 1997). The issue of responsivity to correctional treatment is a crucial but underexplored area in criminological research (but see Birgden, 2004; Bonta, 1995; Ward *et al.*, 2004). Certainly, the topic receives far less attention than identifying risk factors or criminogenic needs.

WHAT IS THE RISK–NEED–RESPONSIVITY MODEL?

Just what constitutes the Risk–Need–Responsivity Model (RNR) is a matter of some debate. Some researchers and practitioners have complained that the model lacks conceptual depth and is essentially a list of principles without theoretical grounding (e.g. Hannah-Moffat, 1999; Ward and Brown, 2003). Critics argue that it is, therefore, incapable of providing correctional personnel with the comprehensive guidance required to reintegrate offenders. Proponents of the RNR model have responded to such criticisms by arguing that a strong theoretical basis exists for this influential rehabilitation model and that once this is clearly articulated the many criticisms fail to hit their mark (e.g. Andrews and Bonta, 2003; Bonta and Andrews, 2003; Ogloff and Davis, 2004). While advocates of the RNR model accept that the theory is often presented purely in terms of the principles of risk, need and responsivity, they claim that this does not mean that it lacks theoretical grounding (e.g. Bonta, 2003). In other words, it is asserted that it is a mistake to frame the RNR model purely in terms of the three rehabilitation principles and the associated program elements. Rather, it is claimed that the theory contained in Andrews and Bonta's seminal book *The Psychology of Criminal Conduct* (2003) and in accompanying articles effectively grounds the three principles, and by doing so outlines a powerful rehabilitation theory.

The trouble with this response is that at least three different theoretical models or perspectives have been presented as providing an underlying theoretical justification for the RNR model. In other words, it is not clear exactly what theory is being appealed to in this debate. First, in their exposition of the RNR model, Ogloff and Davis (2004) proposed that the Psychology of Criminal Conduct perspective (PCC) outlined by Andrews and Bonta (2003) in a number of publications "provides directions for the assessment of offenders and their classification for treatment" (p. 232). Second, Andrews and Bonta (2003) affirm that a model they call a General Personality and Social Psychological Perspective on Criminal Conduct (GPSPP) is able to account for "multiple routes to involvement in illegal conduct" (p. 165). Third, Gillis (2000) asserts that the Personal Interpersonal Community-Reinforcement Perspective (PIC-R) affords a theoretical source for predicting and explaining criminal behavior. Moreover, these three models are all to be found in Andrews and Bonta's discussion of the theoretical underpinnings of their approach to offender rehabilitation in chapters 1 and 4 of *The Psychology of*

Criminal Conduct. For Andrews and Bonta, the three models are thought to provide theoretical support and justification for the "big" three rehabilitation principles of risk, need and responsivity (Bonta, 2003). While all three models are discussed in Andrews and Bonta's (and other RNR proponents') writings, the degree to which they – collectively or individually – can ground the three principles of risk, need and responsivity theoretically is unclear. Another area of vagueness concerns the *relationship* between the three models. Should they be hierarchically related or are they simply alternative conceptualizations of a psychology of criminal conduct? Exactly how should the three models be interrelated within the RNR model of offender rehabilitation?

The difficulty with having more than one theory associated with the RNR model is that it makes the evaluation of the model a difficult and slippery process. It is hard to state exactly what etiological claims are being made and how the principles comprising the RNR model are derived from underlying theory and research. In the trail of such vagueness follow problems of falsification and confirmation. How do we know whether the RNR model is an adequate rehabilitation model if we are unsure what its theoretical commitments are? Furthermore, from an intellectual point of view it is important to link coherently the various strands of the justificatory theory to the RNR principles. Indeed, Andrews and Bonta (2003, p. 4) are adamant that "psychology seeks explanations of criminal conduct that are consistent with the findings of systematic observation, rationally organized, and useful to people with practical interests in criminal behavior". They advocate vigorous critical debate on the theoretical, empirical and practical aspects of offender rehabilitation. Their commitment to rational empiricism is admirable and reminds us that it is important never simply to assume the truth of our favored theories, but always to integrate them critically in the pursuit of greater understanding.

Without a clear statement of the theoretical and methodological commitments of the RNR model, it is harder to defend it against the kinds of criticism outlined above. In order to conclude whether or not they are reasonable it is first necessary to delineate the assumptions of the RNR model in a systematic and coherent manner. Our aim in this chapter is to *reconstruct* the rehabilitation theory in which the three principles of risk, needs and responsivity are implicitly embedded. This task is essentially an architectural one and will involve a careful reading of RNR theoretical work and some degree of redesigning the theory in light of this process of critical reflection. We do not wish to be presumptuous or to claim that this reconstruction represents a new theory or is ours in any significant respect. Rather, our intention is to draw together the various strands of theory from Andrews and Bonta's work and additional theories, and to weave them together in a more systematic and transparent way. Indeed, our hope is that the reconstructed theory will be a stronger and more coherent rehabilitation theory. Our reconstruction of the RNR model concentrates on treatment, but a case could be made for extending it to all interventions in the criminal justice area (see Ward and Yates, 2006).

THEORETICAL SOURCE MODELS OF RNR

There are at least three related but seemingly distinct theoretical models that are associated with the RNR model: the Psychology of Criminal Conduct Perspective (PCC), the General Personality and Social Psychological Perspective on Criminal Conduct (GPSPP) and the Personal Interpersonal Community-Reinforcement Perspective (PIC-R). We shall briefly review each of these models before drawing from all three in our reconstruction of the RNR model. To foreshadow our argument, we suggest that the three models are hierarchically linked (as alluded to in Andrews and Bonta, 2003), with the PCC providing a general set of assumptions concerning the explanation and modification of criminal conduct, the GPSPP sketching out the general contours of an explanatory theory, and the PIC-R in effect fleshing out the GPSPP. That is, the PIC-R is more specific than the GPSPP (see below). They range in order of abstraction from a rather general view of crime to a specific theory centered on dynamic and static risk factors and learning principles (see Figure 3.1).

It is important to note that, although Andrews and Bonta (2003) refer to these models as perspectives, they also refer to them as etiological models or theories in a number of places throughout the book. Therefore, we shall treat them as theories or models rather than as broad perspectives on criminal behavior (we use the terms "models" and "theories" interchangeably). This interpretation is strengthened by Andrews and Bonta's frequent reference to rational empiricism and theory development throughout *The Psychology of Criminal Conduct* (2003). This indicates that one of their aims is to construct a theoretically robust explanation of criminal behavior that is able to ground offender rehabilitation.

PSYCHOLOGY OF CRIMINAL CONDUCT (PCC)

PCC is essentially an approach to the study of criminal conduct based on the investigation of individual differences in the propensity to commit crimes (Andrews, 1995). It describes an *orientation* to the study of crime by identifying psychological correlates of offending. According to Andrews and Bonta (2003), crime is caused by distinct patterns of social and psychological factors that increase the chances that a given individual will break the law. They assert that once the causes of crime have been identified they can be explicitly targeted in order to decrease reoffending rates.

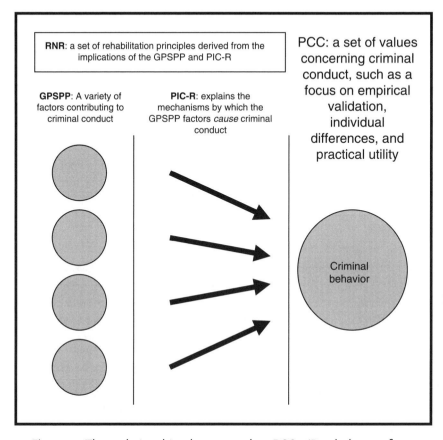

Figure 3.1 The relationship between the PCC (Psychology of Criminal Conduct), the GPSPP (General Personality and Social Psychological Perspective on Criminal Conduct), and the PIC-R (Personal Interpersonal Community-Reinforcement Perspective)

Furthermore, it is assumed that individuals vary in their predisposition to commit deviant acts and that this should be taken into account when planning rehabilitation programs; treatment should be tailored to meet each individual's unique cluster of causes. In other words, the claim is that there exists a "general personality and social psychology of antisocial behavior" that is capable of explaining crime (Andrews and Bonta, 2003, p. 2).

The following two paragraphs capture nicely what Andrews and Bonta (2003) mean by a psychological approach to the explanation and modification of criminal conduct:

> As a science, the psychology of criminal conduct is an approach to understanding the criminal behavior of individuals through: (a) the ethical and humane application of systematic empirical methods of investigation, and (b) the construction of rational explanatory systems.
>
> (p. 15)

> Professionally, a psychology of criminal conduct involves the ethical application of psychological knowledge and methods to the practical tasks of predicting and influencing the likelihood of criminal behavior, and to the reduction of the human and social costs associated with crime and criminal justice processing.
>
> (p. 15)

Thus, the aims of a psychological approach to crime research reflect this focus on individual differences and empirical rigor, and are evident in a number of methodological, theoretical and ethical assumptions. First, there is a focus on variation within individuals and between individuals. The search for such differences should be multifactorial and involve biological, social, cultural, situational and psychological variables. Andrews and Bonta (2003) state that "it is an empirical focus on individual variation in criminal conduct that is the key to PCC, rather than disciplinary or political preferences regarding the potential covariates that ought to be observed" (p. 55). There should be a respect for individual diversity and the complexity of human behavior. Second, researchers seek an empirical understanding of crime through the detection of *co-variates* (i.e. correlates, predictors, and causal or functional variables) using appropriate research designs. These will involve cross-sectional (correlates), longitudinal (predictors), multi-wave longitudinal (dynamic predictors or criminogenic needs) and experimental research designs (functional variables). Third, once empirical regularities have been identified, they argue that it is important to construct sound theoretical explanations of crime. The markers of a sound explanation are what we have called epistemic values: simplicity, internal consistency, external consistency, empirical adequacy and scope, explanatory depth, and practical utility. Fourth, it is stipulated that researchers should hold certain attitudes toward research that take into account the previous assumptions. They should be *open* to new ideas and possible sources of crime co-variates and not dismiss possible knowledge simply because it comes from another discipline. *Theoreticism*, or the dismissal of empirical findings because of fixed ideological positions or self-interest, is regarded as particularly serious and unwarranted. In their depiction of PCC, Andrews and Bonta insist that the research and practical activities of psychologists should be undertaken in ethical and humane ways. Finally, the authors are adamant that in order to advance the understanding of crime and its co-variates it is necessary to engage in "unsparing criticism of theoretical assertions and research findings" (2003, p. 1), albeit criticism that is tempered by a respect for the facts and methods consistent with a scientific approach.

Despite their endorsement of rational empiricism, or perhaps because of it (!), Andrews and Bonta display a laudable tolerance for the social and context dependence of knowledge. More especially they acknowledge the partialness, social, historical and political conditions that constrain the generation of scientific theories and accept that all knowledge is socially constructed. However, this simply serves to underline the fact that theories are formulated by human beings and does not in any way infer that there are no truths to be discovered or a world that cannot be accurately mapped by our best theories.

GENERAL PERSONALITY AND SOCIAL PSYCHOLOGICAL PERSPECTIVE ON CRIMINAL CONDUCT (GPSPP)

The PCC model outlined above is clearly not a comprehensive rehabilitation theory or a detailed etiological model. It is essentially a set of assumptions concerning methodology, theory, research and practice used to inform the study and modification of criminal conduct. As noted above, we use the term "model" loosely when referring to PCC, but in a way that is consistent with Andrews and Bonta's (2003) discussion.

GPSPP, on the other hand, represents a broad theoretical framework guided by the assumptions of PCC. It is Andrews and Bonta's general sketch of the type of explanatory theory that is able to account for crime in a scientifically defensible manner. GPSPP is a complex theory of criminal behavior based on a number of cognitive, behavioral, biological and situational factors. It is based on the diversity evident in biology, personality, cognition, behavioral history and interpersonal functioning in a variety of domains (see Andrews and Bonta, 2003; Bonta, 2000). Most importantly, it is built around the best-established *risk factors* for criminal offending: antisocial cognition, antisocial associates, a history of antisocial behavior, and features of antisocial personality (e.g. impulsivity, poor problem-solving, hostility and callousness). Thus, with GPSPP, Andrews and Bonta seek to construct an explanatory framework that is responsive to the established facts concerning criminal behavior. While they are aware that GPSPP does not provide any detailed description of the putative causal mechanisms, they resist the claim that it is simply a list of risk factors.

In contrast to criminological explanations that propose that the individual's only important characteristic is his/her place in the social system, GPSPP attempts to provide a comprehensive or holistic model of the causes of criminal behavior (Andrews and Bonta, 2003; Ogloff and Davis, 2004). Consistent with PCC, this feature highlights its multifactorial nature; criminal conduct is viewed as having a variety of causes. While the full variety of causes of criminal conduct is acknowledged, it is important to note that GPSPP is primarily a personality and social-learning perspective (Ogloff and Davis, 2004), and draws on an empirical research base suggesting that personality constructs (such as low self-control) and social-learning constructs (such as antisocial peer groups) contribute independently to the generation of criminal behavior (Andrews and Bonta, 2003; Andrews, Bonta and Wormith, 2006).

According to GPSPP, three sets of causal factors (in no particular order) each independently result in an individual defining a high-risk situation in a way that favors the option of committing a crime versus desisting from a crime. The first set of causal factors is the *immediate situation* or what we have termed the high-risk situation. Andrews and Bonta argue that action is subject to powerful situational determinants, and that the cues and potential rewards in immediate situations can facilitate (or the costs inhibit) offending: i.e. when the balance of rewards outweighs the costs. A number of psychological mechanisms derived from different theories are listed as possible mediators of this appraisal process. These include the constructs of behavioral intentions, self-efficacy and neutralization. There is no specification of the mechanisms in any detail, and a number of possibilities are canvassed, primarily involving the array of other causes outlined in the model, such as antisocial cognitions, peer influence and self-management deficits.

The second causal factor is the presence of *delinquent associates* or a peer group who actively support the antisocial behavior of the individual. The exact mechanisms for this influence again are not spelled out but could involve social pressure, reinforcement, adoption of group norms, or simply the fact that the individual's social environment is constrained by the illegal activities and opportunities associated with his or her social network (Andrews and Bonta, 2003).

The third type of cause is the individual's *crime supportive* attitudes, values, beliefs and emotions. These attitudes have been shown to be strongly associated with offending and if modified result in lowered recidivism rates (Andrews and Bonta, 2003). Other causal factors outlined in GPSPP but not directly linked to offending are variables such as early childhood experiences, family of origin, gender, age, ethnicity, school performance and conduct, and a cluster of personality features (e.g. impulsivity or lack of social skills). The other cluster of factors are thought by Andrews and Bonta causally to influence offending in some unspecified manner or through their impact on the three direct routes described above. Importantly, all the factors listed in GPSPP have been identified by research as co-variates of crime (Andrews and Bonta, 2003; Andrews, Bonta and Wormith, 2006; Andrews *et al.*, 1990).

As a theoretical framework, GPSPP only begins to sketch out the set of causal factors associated with crime without any attempt to specify the mechanisms in sufficient detail. It is also apparent that from the perspective of GPSPP there are a number of possible pathways leading to offending depending on the particular cluster of psychological vulnerabilities exhibited by individuals and also the features of the contexts in question. As an etiological theory it is too general to provide a comprehensive explanation of criminal conduct satisfactorily. The fact that it is so flexible and has the ability to incorporate new ideas as research uncovers them raises the possibility that it is not falsifiable. A theory should generate specific predictions and explanatory accounts. If you can simply add new components at will (as new research emerges), then it is not saying anything specific. Furthermore, the lack of clarity (and detail) on the various causal factors (e.g. immediate situation, antisocial cognitions) and their interrelationships means that it is not always clear exactly what is being claimed or why. The primary value of GPSPP, then, seems to rest on its status as a *framework theory*, able to guide the formulation of *substantive* theories for specific types of crime (e.g. sexual or violent offending).

PERSONAL INTERPERSONAL COMMUNITY-REINFORCEMENT PERSPECTIVE (PIC-R)

The third model outlined by Andrews and Bonta (2003) in their influential book *The Psychology of Criminal Conduct* is PIC-R, which argues that the probability of an individual engaging in criminal behavior "is a direct function of the patterns of communication or types of behavior patterns that are modeled, rehearsed, and reinforced to the offender" (Dowden and Andrews, 2004, p. 203). In other words, "offenders need to have anticriminal behavior and/or sentiments modeled and appropriately reinforced for correctional treatment to be effective" (ibid).

This is essentially a fleshed-out version of GPSPP and is the only model that really provides detail concerning the mechanisms that initiate and maintain criminal behavior in the RNR canon. It is important to note that PIC-R is only one of a possible number of models that could be derived from GPSPP depending on how the various risk factors are unpacked and what particular theories are used to explicate the casual mechanisms involved. In fact, Andrews and Bonta (2003) describe this model as "one example of the general personality and social psychological approach" (p. 165) to account for deviant behavior.

In essence PIC-R accepts the array of causal factors outlined in GPSPP but provides more detail on some of them. Thus, social and personal circumstances, interpersonal relationships of various kinds, psychological factors such as self-regulation deficits, personality, and pro-crime cognitions are thought to interact with the immediate situation to result in criminal activity. In addition, it incorporates broad social and cultural factors into the background conditions that confront offenders and constrain their learning opportunities, which ultimately provide conditions that are conducive to criminal activity. PIC-R leans heavily on radical behavioral and social-learning theories with some elements from personality and social psychology also thrown into the mix. Thus, Andrews and Bonta state that PIC-R

> ... emphasizes behavioral and social learning principles because of their demonstrated functional power in applied settings. The practical and clinical utility of the PIC-R will reside in its ability to encourage comprehensive assessments and to assist in planning reasonable and effective interventions.
>
> (pp. 166–7)

In total, Andrews and Bonta unpack PIC-R in terms of fifteen principles that revolve around the behavioral explanation of criminal behavior. It is the detailed description of the learning principles listed, in particular, that gives this model its greater specificity and explanatory power.

A key assumption of PIC-R is that criminal behavior is

acquired and maintained through a combination of operant and classical conditioning, and observational learning (see also Akers, 1998; Sutherland, 1947). The theory states that individuals can adopt antisocial attitudes, goals and behaviors through their association with people who fail to inhibit antisocial behavior (not necessarily offenders). If antisocial behavior is reinforced through rewards or escape from painful stimuli, it is likely to be strengthened and become part of a person's general repertoire in the future. Immediate situations can directly control behavior via the number of rewards and costs contained in them, in conjunction with the contingencies that occur in particular settings. In addition to direct experience, individuals also learn from observing other people and noticing whether their actions are punished or reinforced. A good example of social learning in a criminal context is when a young man watches his father "solve" interpersonal conflicts through the use of violence, resulting in him using the same tactics as an adult. The exposure to the father's aggressive actions is likely to inculcate attitudes favorable to interpersonal violence in the son, and his own subsequent history of rewards and costs for behaving violently in conjunction with the other influences in his life may culminate in the son becoming a violent offender. It is important to note that from the perspective of PIC-R observational learning is only one relevant cause and, generally speaking, multiple causal factors determine whether or not criminal behavior occurs (e.g. reinforcement, the presence of crime-supportive cognitions, etc.).

PIC-R is a more obvious candidate for an explanatory theory of crime but still has limitations. For one thing, the processes associated with the different risk factors are not fleshed out and it is not clear what mechanisms actually comprise dynamic risk factors such as antisocial peers or self-management problems. The relationship between the various risk factors is also a little vague and requires further elucidation. The details that are provided concerning the operation of radical behavioral and social-learning principles apply to any behavior and are not specific to any particular type of offending. Most importantly, however, what is provided in PIC-R is a collection of variable names and their possible relationships. The problem of explaining how the risk factors actually operate and influence criminal actions is left unaddressed. In short, PIC-R is a little undercooked and would benefit from further elaboration indicating how causal elements such as antisocial attitudes or personality features generate particular types of antisocial behavior in specific settings (e.g. sexual or violent offenses).

REHABILITATION IMPLICATIONS

The primary treatment implication of these models is that interventions ought to be focused on modifying or eliminating dynamic risk factors (criminogenic needs). It is noteworthy that, consistent with the broad orientation of the three models, this includes individual, social and ecological/environmental factors. From the standpoints of PCC, GPSPP and PIC-R, criminogenic needs represent clinical needs that are stipulated to be the primary targets of rehabilitation effects. Thus, the whole rehabilitation process is recommended to be driven by the empirical detection of the correlates of crime rather than treatment targets being simply derived in an *a priori* fashion from clinical or criminological theories without a consideration of research findings.

What is lacking, however, is clear guidance on what to "do" about criminogenic needs or risk factors once identified. Practitioners are instructed to "target", "tackle" and "address" various deficits, yet given little by way of guidance on what this entails. As such, the three theories that have been postulated as underlying the RNR model are unable to supply the necessary etiological and theoretical components to ground a model of offender rehabilitation. First, the models on their own lack the resources to justify the core assumptions of the RNR model with respect to the notion of risk, need and responsivity. For example, PCC is primarily concerned with outlining what we have referred to as the first component (values, aims, etc.) of a rehabilitation theory and is vague when it comes to etiology. While GPSPP and PIC-R are better able to deal with the etiological aspects (with varying degrees of success), they fail to articulate the values and broad assumptions underpinning the RNR model. Second, it is unclear whether the RNR model is essentially a rehabilitation theory or simply a cluster of principles. There is a certain ambiguity in the way the term "RNR model" has been used by researchers. On the one hand, it refers to the three principles of risk, need and responsivity and their accompanying program assumptions (see below). On the other hand, it refers to the three principles, the components of an effective program, and the theoretical and methodological assumption contained in the three source models. In other words, there is considerable vagueness concerning what comprises the RNR model. What is needed is a systematic exposition of the RNR model incorporating the three components or levels of a rehabilitation described earlier.

THE RECONSTRUCTED RISK–NEED–RESPONSIVITY MODEL

We shall now attempt to *reconstruct* the RNR rehabilitation theory by drawing upon the collective resources of the three models and the principles of risk, need and responsivity (plus other elements of effective service programming). Our aim is to present the RNR model in its strongest possible form in order to evaluate more accurately its strengths and weaknesses. Note that by the term "RNR model" we are referring to the *entire rehabilitation theory*, not simply the three classification principles and their accompanying program components. In other words, we accept the claim by major proponents of the RNR model (e.g. Andrews and Bonta, 2003) that it is a comprehensive rehabilitation framework theory rather than a collection of principles and a few assumptions. Our job in this section is to reconstruct the RNR model component by component (see Figure 3.2).

It should be noted that the formulation of the RNR model and the three source theories in Andrews and Bonta's various published works are rather general and tentative in places, and therefore at times we have had to make judgments about their meaning (e.g. concerning the relationship between the three models or the way risk is conceptualized).

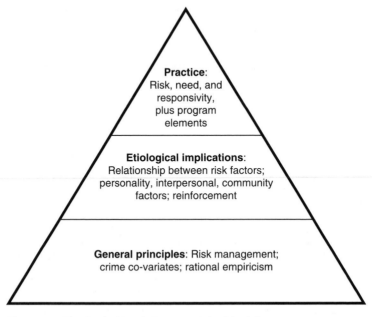

Practice:
Risk, need, and
responsivity,
plus program
elements

Etiological implications:
Relationship between risk factors;
personality, interpersonal, community
factors; reinforcement

General principles: Risk management;
crime co-variates; rational empiricism

Figure 3.2 The Risk–Need–Responsivity Model

Thus, our depiction of the RNR model is a reconstruction in two senses: (*a*) it represents a reformulation of the RNR model using the three-component structure outlined earlier; and (*b*) it embodies our own interpretations of the various source models, including the creative filling of previously identified gaps.

PRINCIPLES, AIMS AND VALUES

There are a number of basic assumptions that constitute the first level or component of the RNR rehabilitation model. First, the primary aim of offender rehabilitation is to reduce the amount of harm inflicted on members of the public and on society by offenders. Considerations of the offender's welfare are secondary to this, with the caveat that any interventions must not intentionally harm him unnecessarily or violate commonly accepted professional ethical standards (see McCord, 2003). It is acknowledged that there is always some degree of harm experienced by an offender during therapy (e.g. feelings of distress or shame), but this is typically viewed as relatively minor and necessary to achieve therapy goals.

Second, individuals are likely to vary with respect to their predisposition to commit crimes. The factors that are associated with offending come from a range of variables including biological, psychological, social, cultural, personal, interpersonal and situational factors. Research into offending should be broad in scope. Furthermore, effective treatment requires that clinicians have systematically assessed offenders and identified their particular risk factors and offense pathways.

Third, the severity of risk (i.e. whether low, medium or high) is assumed to co-vary with the number of criminogenic needs, and additionally with the severity or strength of each need. That is, lower-risk individuals will have few, if any, criminogenic needs while higher-risk individuals will display a significant range of such needs. Risk factors are viewed as discrete, quantifiable characteristics of individuals and their environments that can be identified and measured. The conceptualization of risk is from the individualist perspective.

Fourth, the most important treatment targets are those characteristics that research has associated with potentially reduced recidivism rates. Everything else is, at best, of marginal relevance and, at worst, potentially obstructive and harmful. The key issue here is that it is important to use the scarce resources available to manage crime to best effect, which means reducing the empirically established triggers of offending where possible. Above all, a risk-management rehabilitation perspective is concerned with reducing the likelihood that individuals will engage in behavior that will prove harmful to the community. The expectation is that by identifying and managing dynamic risk factors (e.g. antisocial attitudes and impulsivity) offending rates will be reduced. Fifth, the identification of risk factors and/or criminogenic needs is said to be an empirical and therefore value-free process. Note this does not mean that values are not involved in rehabilitation; simply that the detection of crime co-variates is value-free. The detection of correlates of crime should be undertaken with rigor and appropriate research designs; and, while it is accepted that knowledge is always partial and subject to social and political interests, it is possible to acquire an accurate understanding of the causes of crime. Relatedly, using the knowledge of the causes of crime it is possible to design effective treatment programs.

Sixth, individuals should be treated humanely, with research and treatment delivered in an ethically responsible manner. Considerations of responsivity and motivation alongside respect for basic human rights mean that offenders should be regarded as persons who have the capacity to change their behavior. Still, as stated above, the primary aim of offender rehabilitation should be to reduce the risk to society rather than to enhance the well-being of offenders. This is really an issue of priority, and it is not assumed that offenders' welfare is unimportant or incompatible with the promotion of community safety.

ETIOLOGICAL AND METHODOLOGICAL ASSUMPTIONS

In the components of the RNR model of offender rehabilitation there are a number of etiological and methodological assumptions drawn primarily from GPSPP and PIC-R. First, there are a number of major risk factors (known as the "big eight") for offending and these are causally linked to criminal conduct or at least function as indicators of causes: antisocial attitudes, antisocial associates, a history of antisocial behavior, antisocial personality pattern, problematic circumstances at home, difficulties at work or at school, problems with leisure activities, and substance abuse. An empirically informed etiological theory of crime should be based on these risk factors and outline their relationships to each other (where known) and actual incidents of crime. Thus, theory construction is a *bottom-up* process in the sense that theoretical constructs are constrained by the detection of empirical regularities. There is nothing sacrosanct about the big eight, and the exact number of risk factors should always reflect the findings of research, and variation according to predictors of the type of crime (e.g. sexual offending versus property crime). It is critical that researchers are open to new findings and that the resultant theories display the epistemic values of simplicity, internal consistency, external consistency, empirical adequacy and scope, explanatory depth and practical utility.

The proximal cause of offending is the framing of an

immediate (high-risk) situation in such a way that the rewards of criminal activity are evaluated as outweighing the costs. Rewards are viewed as plural in nature and range from the automatic and physiologically based reinforcement of drug ingestion to social acceptance and approval from other offenders. It is not clear what psychological mechanisms actually mediate the process of reward/cost appraisal. According to the RNR model, the possible mechanisms include self-efficacy expectations, intentions, or perception of the density of rewards in a situation. Thus, there is room for a phenomenological (based on subjective awareness and conscious intentions) or a more mechanistic explanation. The presence of delinquent associates (external) and crime-supportive attitudes, values and beliefs distorts the appraisal process and increases the chances that certain individuals commit an offense in a specific situation. Further factors such as social rejection or disconnection, relationship problems and ongoing self-management deficits make it more likely that the antisocial cognitions of certain individuals will be activated and that they will be susceptible to the influence of delinquent peers.

More distal causes of an individual's predisposition to experience the problems outlined above include developmental adversity (e.g. sexual or physical abuse, neglect) and growing up in an environment in which antisocial norms have been modeled, or where the opportunities to lead a crime-free life are significantly low. Once a crime has been committed its effects are likely to reinforce further offending and the individual concerned will be responsive to environmental and internal cues that signal the presence of offending opportunities. In fact, according to the RNR model, environments exert a powerful influence on behavior. Andrews and Bonta argue that in order to explain fully the likelihood that a person will perpetrate a crime it is also essential to consider the wider political, economic and cultural contexts within which he or she lives. However, these conditions alone are insufficient to *cause* crime – the individual/personal factors must also be present. Andrews and Bonta argue strongly that, while political, economic and cultural conditions may set the stage for criminal actions, antisocial learning and attitudes, and the other causal elements outlined in the RNR model, mediate these broad effects.

The RNR model therefore contains an integrated set of etiological assumptions and accompanying methodological commitments. It is a multidimensional and dynamic theoretical approach that respects empirical evidence but is also sensitive to the social ecological and cultural contexts of offending.

PRACTICE IMPLICATIONS

The theory above lays out the necessary groundwork for the well-known principles of risk, need and responsivity central to the RNR model. First, the *risk* principle is concerned with the match between individuals' level of risk for reoffending and the amount of treatment/interventions they should receive. The assumption is that risk is a rough indicator of clinical need and, therefore, according to this principle, high-risk individuals should receive the most treatment, typically at least 100 hours of cognitive behavioral interventions (Hollin, 1999). Those individuals displaying moderate levels of risk should receive a lesser dose of treatment, while those designated as low-risk warrant little, if any, intervention. Risk can be divided into static and dynamic risk factors. Static risk factors are variables that cannot be changed, for example, number of past offenses or gender. Dynamic risk factors are attributes of the individual or of his or her situation that are able to be modified in some important respects, for example, impulsivity or deviant sexual preferences. Furthermore, an important assumption is that the severity of risk (i.e. whether low, medium or high) is likely to co-vary with the intensity and depth of the criminogenic needs present.

Second, according to the *need* principle, treatment programs should primarily focus on changing criminogenic needs – that is, dynamic characteristics that, when changed, are associated with reduced recidivism rates (e.g. impulsiveness or poor problem-solving abilities). Although clinicians may sometimes decide to treat noncriminogenic needs (e.g. depression or grief) in therapy, they should not expect these efforts to result in lower recidivism rates. For example, setting out to enhance an individual's self-esteem may leave him or her feeling better about themselves but, according to Andrews and Bonta (2003), will not (on its own) reduce reoffending rates. In fact, according to some research, targeting such variables may in fact increase individuals' chances of reoffending (Baumeister, 1999; Ogloff and Davis, 2004).

Third, the *responsivity* principle is used to refer to the use of a style and mode of intervention that engages the interest of the client group and takes into account their relevant characteristics such as cognitive ability, learning style, and values (Andrews and Bonta, 2003). The responsivity principle states that treatment strategies should be carefully matched to the preferred learning styles of the treatment recipient (Andrews and Bonta, 2003). Bonta (1995) argues that treatment effectiveness depends on matching types of treatment and therapist to types of client based on the personal "styles" of both.

Internal responsivity is related to the need to attend to individual circumstances and a particular array of causes, and cautions clinicians to view each offender as an individual rather than adopt "a one size fits all" approach. External responsivity signals the importance of ensuring that features of the interventions utilized and the contexts in which they are implemented are taken into account. Offender motivation, gender and cultural issues are all important features explicitly to consider when adjusting therapy to individuals' particular features and situations.

Clearly, all three principles (risk, need and responsivity) depend entirely on the comprehensive and empirically validated assessment of correctional clients. To help in this process, Andrews and Bonta (1995) developed the Level of Service Inventory – Revised (LSI-R), a 54-item measure that addresses a wide range of static and dynamic variables associated with criminal conduct. The domains covered by the LSI-R instrument include: offending history, education, employment, family and marital relationships, accommodation, friendships, the use of alcohol and drugs, emotional problems, and attitudes toward offending. Instruments such as LSI-R and measures of risk are used to allocate individuals to treatment programs and to determine the necessary intensity or "dose" of treatment.

Second, in conjunction with the RNR principles outlined earlier, Andrews and Bonta (2003) stress that there are six main principles needed for effective rehabilitation. They argue that treatment programs should be: (1) cognitive-behavioral in orientation; (2) highly structured, specifying the aims and tasks to be covered in each session; (3) implemented by trained, qualified and appropriately supervised staff; (4) delivered in the intended manner and as intended by program developers to ensure treatment integrity; (5) manual based; and (6) housed within institutions with personnel committed to the ideals of rehabilitation and a management structure (i.e. key correctional personnel and policies within an agency) that supports rehabilitation (Andrews and Bonta, 2003; Gendreau and Andrews, 1990; Gendreau, Goggin, Cullen and Andrews, 2000; Gendreau, Little and Goggin, 1996; Hollin, 1999; McGuire, 2002; Ogloff and Davis, 2004).

Finally, researchers and theorists are continuing to

strengthen the RNR model. One area of current interest is that of responsivity, including the problem of motivation. In particular, Ogloff and Davis (2004) have made some valuable suggestions for improving treatment outcome by addressing *responsivity impediments* such as acute mental illness and lack of motivation. They suggest that these problems can adversely impact on individuals' ability to behave autonomously and therefore should be dealt with before embarking on treatment targeting criminogenic needs. Furthermore, Ogloff and Davis recommend that, following sufficient progress in reducing criminogenic needs, efforts can be made to enhance individuals' well-being and therefore help them to adopt ways of living that will prove more satisfying (see the next two chapters) than a criminal lifestyle.

CONCLUSIONS

In this chapter we have tried to present RNR in its strongest-possible form. This has meant that we have undertaken some reconstructive work and had to make a number of decisions about what to include in the model description and at what level (i.e. components A, B or C). It is clear that RNR is built around a risk framework and that the notion of offender "need" plays a secondary role at most in the process of rehabilitation (Hannah-Moffat, 2005). It is an indisputable fact that RNR is among the premier rehabilitation models in operation today, and the model has an impressive research record to back up its claims. Yet, despite its obvious merits, there are areas of concern and there are nagging doubts about its ability to provide correctional workers with the guidance they require in the difficult process of helping individuals turn their lives around. In the next chapter we shall attempt to address these lingering concerns about the theoretical adequacy of the RNR model.

4

EVALUATING THE RISK–NEED–RESPONSIVITY MODEL

In the correctional field, the shift to a risk-management perspective, and the focus of therapeutic efforts on the modification of acute and dynamic risk factors, means that the RNR model is the premier rehabilitation theory in existence in the world today. Andrews, Bonta and Wormith (2006) argue that "theoretical, empirical, and applied progress within the psychology of criminal conduct (PCC) has been nothing less than revolutionary" (p. 8) and that "The general personality and social psychology of crime . . . is now the prominent theoretical position in criminology" (p. 9). Certainly, the model has led to a wide range of research initiatives on risk assessment and treatment techniques for diverse offender groups, and has been central in "saving" rehabilitation as an ideal (Cullen, 2005).

Despite this clear success, aspects of the RNR model remain underdeveloped and vulnerable to criticism. In this chapter, we constructively interrogate the theoretical, empirical and clinical utility of this extremely influential rehabilitation theory. Our strategy will follow that outlined in Chapter 2: each of the three components will be scrutinized focusing on the RNR model's strengths or weaknesses and then an overall evaluation of the model will be made.

One important preliminary point is that what constitutes RNR is a matter of some debate. In our view, the reconstructed RNR sketched in the last chapter represents the theory in its strongest form, and therefore we have chosen to evaluate this version rather than one of the other available (less explicitly developed) versions. In doing so, we are aware that many of the criticisms previously made against RNR, some of which we formulated ourselves (e.g. Ward and Brown, 2004; Ward and Stewart, 2003), may no longer hold. Therefore, in this chapter we focus only on what we consider to be the strengths and weaknesses of the *reconstructed* model.

The three components of the RNR model of offender rehabilitation are as follows: (a) basic assumptions and values, (b) etiological assumptions and (c) practice implications. To reiterate our earlier point, the three components are linked in a stepwise way; the basic assumptions and values partially determine what kinds of explanation of crime are sought, and the type of interventions utilized depends in part on correctional agencies' stipulated interests and the favored etiological theories.

BASIC ASSUMPTIONS AND VALUES

RNR contains a set of primary assumptions and values concerning the model's basic metaphysical, epistemological and ethical commitments. The articulation of these underlying assumptions and values effectively underpins the etiological commitments of RNR and focuses research activities on what are considered to be high-priority tasks; for example, the identification of the co-variates of crime. This is aided by a depiction of risk in *individualist* terms as independent, quantifiable factors that can be reliably measured and incorporated into risk-prediction procedures. Thus, the etiological component and practice guidelines of RNR make sense in light of the assumptions and values contained in component one (i.e. the first level of the RNR model – see last chapter). This is a strength of the model and points to its internal coherence. In addition, the inclusion of some ethical and prudential values helps practitioners and researchers to ensure that their activities do not unduly harm individuals or contravene their rights. This feature of RNR indicates its external consistency with accepted practice.

However, there are also a number of aspects of RNR that are still in need of development. These typically relate to the theory's rather singular focus on risk and at times poorly articulated assumptions. Each will be discussed below.

Values and the Risk–Need–Responsivity model. One criticism concerns the role of values more generally in the RNR model and the relationship of criminogenic needs to values or normative issues. Although there is attention to epistemological and ethical values in RNR, it is rather narrowly drawn. The impression is that values are viewed as equivalent to subjective preferences of individuals, along the lines of taste preferences for certain foods. In our view this is a mistake. There is a robust and developing literature in a variety of research domains indicating that there are certain (valued) conditions that increase people's level of well-being and reduce their chances of experiencing harm (e.g. Arnhart, 1998; Aspinwall and Staudinger, 2003; Braybrooke, 1987; Deci and Ryan, 2000; Emmons, 1999; Murphy, 2001; Nussbaum; 2000; Thomson, 1987). Basic human needs are examples of motives that incline individuals to seek types of experiences and objects, outcomes that objectively result in greater physical health and well-being. To the extent that these needs are based in facts, they should be understood as "objective" and not simply subjective preferences (see also Ashford, Sales and Reid, 2001).

Conceptualization of need. A related point concerns the relationship between criminogenic needs and values. The fact that criminogenic needs are partially defined in terms of their relationship to harmful and beneficial outcomes indicates that they are *value-laden* terms. The assumption is that if criminogenic needs are targeted in treatment, then less harm and greater good will accrue to society. The difficulty is that "harm" and "good" are value-laden terms and therefore the RNR model does presuppose normative judgments concerning what is beneficial to the community and to the offender. In other words, the very notion of risk itself is conceptually tied to subjective ideas of harms and benefits. This is not to say that "anything can be a risk" or that "there is no risk in reality" – social constructionist critiques that Andrews and colleagues (2006) have bristled over in the past. The point is simply that the detection of risk factors involves value judgments alongside the collection of facts, and that, in science and its applications, facts and values are inextricably connected.

Nowhere is the role of values more clear, in fact, than in the RNR conceptualization of "needs" (see Hannah-Moffat, 2005). This Orwellian redefinition of "needs" as the "dynamic attributes of the offender that, when changed, are associated with changes in the probability of recidivism" (Andrews and Bonta, 1998, p. 243) seems to transform the word "needs" into another term for "dynamic risk factors" (as acknowledged by the authors themselves). Hence, one might be treating the "needs" of a sex offender through castration or targeting the needs of a violent offender through capital punishment. Somehow Maslow left such unpalatable outcomes off his famous hierarchy! At any rate, if criminogenic needs are to be equated with risk factors, and noncriminogenic needs are largely neglected or explicitly downplayed in the model, then RNR is clearly weighing risk above need – a clear statement of values.

The conceptualization of risk. It is clear that the notion of risk plays a pivotal role in the RNR model, but somewhat oddly there is little attempt by RNR theorists to articulate the conceptual basis for this concept. This is particularly problematic because in the correctional domain risk has numerous connotations (see Denny, 2005) and is a strongly contested concept (see Robinson, 1999; Sparks, 2001). In addition, the way risk is formulated has clear etiological and practice implications, and therefore it is important to consider explicitly how risk is understood and what its theoretical assumptions are.

Earlier we identified what we considered to be the dominant conceptualization of risk in the correctional arena, the individualist perspective. According to this theory, risk is viewed as consisting of discrete individual characteristics associated with offending behavior and, thus, is thought to exist on an identifiable underlying behavioral continuum ranging from low to high (Brown, 2000). The core idea is that individuals are basically a bundle or cluster of properties that are in principle observable and measurable (e.g. see Hoffman and Beck, 1974, 1985). The methods used to assess risk are analytic and reductionist, enabling clinicians to examine the relationship of specific characteristics to criminal behavior. Risk factors are thought to be susceptible to manipulation and management, and therefore rehabilitation programs set out to target identified risk factors and to teach the offender new, pro-social ways of thinking and acting. The idea is to give individuals the skills necessary to cope with problems in socially acceptable ways.

Other risk theorists have contested the focus on individual characteristics and have argued that cultural, social or phenomenological factors create and maintain perceptions of risk and harmful situations (e.g. Brown, 2000; Gottfredson and Taylor, 1988; Lynch and Sabol, 2001). For example, in his categorical model Brown proposes that risk reflects aspects of human character (e.g. virtue and/or vices). He states that individuals are best-viewed as agents who act upon the world in a manner that expresses aspects of their character. It is this expression of character that enables perceptive observers to estimate whether or not offenders constitute an ongoing risk to themselves or to the community. Thus, risk markers in this view of risk are carefully considered features of human individuality rather than disembodied and atomized "factors" (as in individual risk assessment). A good example of a character-based characteristic relevant to risk assessment is remorse. For risk evaluators relying on the categorical model, remorse is viewed as a virtue indicating that a person truly understands the harm he or she has done. In addition, the presence of remorse reveals a determination to accept responsibility for his or her criminal conduct and a desire to change his or her antisocial inclinations.

Therefore, from the perspective of the categorical model, risk cannot be "measured" in a quantitative manner but can only be assessed through systematic and careful judgment, a holistic and partly intuitive process. Of course, it is well known that actuarial models of risk assessment based on an individualist model of risk are better predictors of future behavior than are clinical judgments (see Gendreau, Goggin and Smith, 2002; Grove *et al.*, 2000). Yet the implications of these models of risk transcend assessment and prediction and strike at the heart of how rehabilitation is practiced (Garland, 2001; but see also the debate between Hans Toch and Leslie Wilkins on this point: Toch and Wilkins, 1985). For instance, the preferred intervention approach of the categorical model is not the packaged cognitive or skills approach characteristic of most contemporary psychological treatment programs but rather assistance in personal development that would allow the individual concerned to reform his or her character, and to experience the appropriate moral emotions. According to Brown (2000), a categorical risk model frequently underlies the assessments of judicial decision-makers and other criminal justice practitioners who reject a quantitative model of risk assessment.

The difficulty is that correctional professionals such as psychologists, correctional officers, policy analysts, and judges rarely acknowledge that they work with contrasting models of risk and therefore often talk at cross-purposes when discussing risk assessment with each other. It is clear to us that the RNR model assumes the validity of the individual or psychometric conception of risk and therefore is most concerned with issues of offender management, and not with questions of value or character (unless the latter are viewed as measurable sources of antisocial behavior). Both models have their basis in broader conceptualizations of the world and of the nature of people.

One of the concerns about adopting an individualist account of risk is that it creates the impression that offenders are intrinsically bearers of risk and that specific risk factors inhere or are embedded in them, a bit like pins in a pincushion. Thus, there can be a failure to appreciate how social and cultural factors on occasion can actively generate high situations of risk and in this sense shape perceptions of risk. For example, laws and policies that legislate intensive monitoring and control of individuals in the community may result in an inability to reintegrate offenders into social networks and to establish adaptive ways of meeting their needs (see Padfield and Maruna, 2006). A risk-aversive society in effect quarantines offenders and by doing so leads to (*a*) exaggerated public fears and anxiety about personal safety, (*b*) social exclusion of individuals with criminal records, and (*c*) increased risk because of offenders' lack of opportunities to pursue rewarding, pro-social lifestyles.

Paradoxically, the combination of social stigmatization and an overly individualist notion of risk can increase the chances that an offender will commit another offense (Beech and Ward, 2004; Hanson and Morton-Bourgon, 2005; Jenkins, 1998).

Contextual/ecological factors in offender rehabilitation. From its origins (especially Andrews, Bonta and Hoge, 1990), the RNR model was promoted as an alternative to the then dominant sociological discourse in criminology that placed poverty, social disadvantage and community at the core of the criminogenic process. Indeed, RNR advocates frequently assemble an array of evidence in arguing for the irrelevance of such factors to individual differences in criminal behaviors. Possibly as a result of this unusual reading of the sociological literature, the RNR model explicitly underplays the contextual nature of human behavior and seeks to build general principles that are applied without much consideration of the local circumstances and macro-economic forces impacting individual lives. Because human beings are interdependent and rely on other people and social institutions to function, care should be taken to ensure any treatment plan takes into account the contexts in which offenders are likely to be released (Ward and Stewart, 2003). For instance, numerous critics have questioned whether RNR-based cognitive treatment programs are "culturally appropriate for the largely inner-city minority populations" (Wilson and Davis, 2006) that comprise the majority of many criminal justice interventions in the US and elsewhere (Hannah-Moffat, 1999). According to this objection, the RNR model is inconsistent (lacks external consistency) with the facts about human functioning and suffers from a lack of practical utility (fertility).

Although the RNR model in its reconstructed form (Chapter 3) does point to the need to consider individuals' personal situations and social networks when formulating an explanation of offending behavior, it does not really make the theoretical basis for this recommendation explicit. Because the focus is on individuals and their potential for harmful behavior, little attention is paid to the interdependency of people. The issue of the ecological validity of the RNR model requires further elaboration.

Risk management policy. RNR's focus on risk management presumes that the major aim of rehabilitation is to reduce the chances of harm to the community and that this is best-achieved by managing these risks. Harmless as this sounds, this assumption can lead to problems if adhered to in a rigid manner. First, it is unclear how an approach *focused* on the prevention of harmful consequences to others can encourage offenders to change their own behavior in fundamental ways. This is really an issue of how best to motivate individuals to engage in therapy (see below). The lack of explicit attention to the question of what motivates offenders (as human beings) means that correctional workers can alienate individuals by focusing exclusively on harm reduction to the community without considering what is of importance to them.

In essence, although reduction of risk to the community is a perfectly valid social aim, it does not translate well into a usable clinical aim when working with individual offenders. What is required at the clinical level is some attention to helping offenders build a better life (not just a less harmful one) in ways that are personally meaningful and satisfying, and socially acceptable. Clients need to "buy in" to a rehabilitation strategy, believe it is the best thing for them and actually want to succeed at it. Concentrating on criminogenic needs is arguably not that helpful to clinicians (and offenders) because it encourages them to focus largely on the elimination or modification of criminogenic needs rather than on how to attain primary human goods.

Personality and personal agency. Another objection is that the RNR model is so concerned with reducing risk and targeting criminogenic needs that there is insufficient attention to the individual as a whole – that is, his or her self-identity. In the RNR model, personality appears to involve little more than one's dispositional traits (e.g. levels of self-control, agreeableness or extraversion). These traits play a central role in the measurement of risk, need and especially responsivity. Yet personality psychologists have long argued that there is more to persons and to personality than our traits (Helson and Stewart, 1994).

In particular, McAdams (1994) has argued that personality should be understood as involving three levels or, more accurately, domains: traits, personal strivings and self-narratives. The first and most basic of these is our traits like impulsivity or introversion. These characteristic ways of behaving are thought to have a strong genetic component, tend to be shaped early in an individual's development, and are unlikely to change substantially over the life course – at least relative to one's age group (see McRae and Costa, 1994). So an adolescent who is relatively wild and adventurous compared to other adolescents will likely grow up to be an elderly person who is also wild and adventurous, but only compared to other elderly persons (not to teenagers or even to his or her adolescent self).

The other two domains of personality (both neglected in the RNR model) tend to be far more dynamic and agentic (that is, at the control of the individual actor). As such, these two levels present the best opportunity for changing personality over the life course (see McAdams, 1994). Individuals' personal strivings express their sense of who they are and what they would like to become (Emmons, 1986). Personality, for offenders and for all people, is at least in part constituted from the pursuit and achievement of these personal goals – regardless of their traits (Bruner, 1990;

Singer, 2005). Predictably, these strivings change over the life course in response to changes in context and normative, social expectations. For example, suppose an individual's personality traits tend toward shyness and a tendency to prefer the familiar to the unknown. If such an individual were to find herself newly divorced, her personality might become suddenly more outgoing as she pursues goals of intimacy and bonding with others. Moreover, her personality might revert to form upon reaching these goals.

The third domain of personality, the narrative identity, may be the most dynamic of all the levels of personality. According to McAdams's theory, modern adults create an internalized life-story – or personal myth – in order to provide their lives with unity, purpose and meaning. The construction and reconstruction of this narrative, integrating one's perceived past, present and anticipated future, is itself the process of identity development in adulthood. Essentially, this is a reflective understanding of an individual's life that captures what is of importance to him or her, and how these commitments evolve over time in response to his or her personal circumstances and the various people he or she is acquainted with. In other words, self-identity is a story with characters, a set of themes, and a plot that unfolds across time in a relatively coherent fashion. The narrative identity can be understood as an active information-processing structure, a cognitive schema, or a construct system that is both shaped by and later mediates social interaction. Essentially, people construct stories to account for what they do and why they did it. These narratives impose an order on our actions and explain our behavior with a sequence of events that connect to explanatory goals, motivations and feelings. These self-narratives then act to shape and guide future behavior, as persons act in ways that agree with the stories or myths we have created about ourselves (Bruner, 1986; McAdams, 1985, 2006).

Considerable therapeutic work, from psychoanalysis to new forms of narrative therapy, is aimed at helping individuals develop more adaptive self-narratives and change their habitual ways of understanding their life, with the assumption that such a shift in worldview will lead to changed behavioral outcomes (Monk *et al.*, 1996). Indeed, there is growing evidence from research in criminology and criminological psychology that development on this level of personality is a facilitative condition for desisting from reoffending. In his research with ex-prisoners, Maruna (2001), for instance, found that individuals needed to establish an alternative, coherent and pro-social self-identity in order to justify and maintain their desistance from crime. This required the construction of a narrative that made sense of their earlier crimes and experiences of adversity and created a bridge between their undesirable lives and new ways of living. Desisting offenders appeared to live according to a *redemption script*, where negative past experiences were reinterpreted as providing a pathway or conduit to the forging of a new identity and more authentic ways of living (for convergent findings, see also Barry, 2006; Giordano *et al.*, 2002; Stefanakis, 1998; Terry, 2002).

In the applied world of rehabilitation, Haaven and Coleman (2000) developed a model for the treatment of developmentally disabled sex offenders based on the construction of a new personal identity. In this model, treatment is based around the distinction between a "new me" and an "old me". The "old me" constitutes the individual who committed sexual offenses and encompasses values, goals, beliefs and ways of living that directly generate offending behavior (i.e. risk factors). The construction of a "new me" involves the endorsement of a new set of goals that specify a "good" life for an individual, that is, a life in which important primary goods are achieved in ways that are socially acceptable and personally fulfilling. The RNR model's lack of attention to the role of personal identity in the change process indicates that it cannot provide adequate guidance to therapists on these unavoidable issues. In other words, offenders' therapeutic progress is causally related to the formation of meaningful personal goals and identity development.

Related to this is a lack of appreciation for personal choice in the setting of treatment goals and the importance of gearing treatment to the needs and interests of offenders while still modifying their level of risk. Thus, the claim is that the RNR model does not pay enough attention to the role of personal or narrative identity and agency (i.e. self-directed, intentional actions designed to achieve valued goals) in the change process. This problem suggests that the RNR model lacks external consistency, unifying power and practical utility (fertility).

It must be noted that the focus in the reconstructed RNR on the etiological components (see below) of the social environment and personal circumstances does provide some conceptual space to expand on the notion of identity. The cultural and broad social contexts of crime also point to the relevance of institutional processes and roles for rehabilitation. An offender's interpersonal environment provides resources and opportunities for his pursuit of personal goals and projects. It provides him or her with the resources and opportunities to pursue what is important to him or her and to consolidate a new, more adaptive sense of identity, of who he or she is. Thus, this is not a fatal objection against the reconstructed theory, and the RNR model may have the theoretical resources to expand on this aspect of treatment.

Assumptions about human nature. The RNR model appears to assume a radical behaviorist view of human nature. Radical behaviorism has commitments to a narrow, minimalist view of human nature, with the emphasis on learning experiences and the acquisition of behavioral repertoires as a function of reinforcement. This assumption appears to restrict the range of rewards that are typically sought by individuals in every sphere of their life, including offending. However, the reconstructed RNR model's flexible structure allows for the introduction of additional theoretical commitments as researchers discover relevant information about human motivation and functioning. Furthermore, the concept of rewards inherent in the RNR model does not preclude primary human goods and human needs. Thus, the open-ended nature of the reconstructed RNR model leaves room for expanding on the role of goods or needs if this is defensible from a scientific point of view. However, this aspect of RNR is underdeveloped and in this sense remains a significant problem.

"What Works" as a normative justification. Finally, the normative grounds on which the RNR model rests need to be scrutinized as well. That is, what in RNR justifies intervention into people's lives in the first place? Although such normative discussions play a minimal role in the RNR literature, this foundation could not be more apparent. RNR is justified on the grounds of "what works". Its empirical justification is its normative justification and vice versa. In other words, the argument seems to be that it is "right" to subject people to RNR interventions because they demonstrably reduce recidivism. This is a utilitarian good for society and arguably even for the individuals themselves (as it will help them avoid future imprisonment and other sanctions).

The problem with such utilitarian justifications, as countless philosophers have argued, is that they would justify even the most extreme interventions (from castration to capital punishment) if they are found to "work". This is where RNR's ethical principles come into play of course (e.g. that clients should be treated decently, with the least possible amount of harm, etc.), but such principles are arguably an inadequate defense against the overwhelming force of "what works".

ETIOLOGICAL ASSUMPTIONS

The etiological commitments of RNR are conceptually related to the major assumptions and values outlined above. The major emphasis on risk assessment and management means that the primary emphasis of the explanatory component of RNR is on identifying criminogenic needs and their origins in learning experiences and social and biological factors.

Conceptual depth. The most substantial criticism of the original RNR model is that it is not a comprehensive theory of rehabilitation but rather is essentially a set of principles that are loosely related. It is important for a rehabilitation theory to function as a bridge between etiological assumptions and the implementation of treatment. Critics charge that there is simply not enough substance to the RNR model to do this adequately (Ward and Stewart, 2003). Because of the way Andrews and Bonta (2003) conceptualize risk (see below), criminogenic needs are derived statistically from large data sets and examined individually for their ability to predict reoffending. Thus, according to the RNR model, each risk factor has its own (statistical) relationship to reoffending and functions somewhat in isolation from the others. In addition, the three source theories underpinning the principles (see Chapter 3) essentially *describe* how developmental, early learning, family relations, school experiences and so on could converge to produce crime-supportive appraisals. They do not go beneath the surface to propose in detail how these variables interact to create different etiological pathways to offending.

The reconstructed RNR model of the last chapter, however, largely negates these criticisms. Still, it remains the case that the reconstructed RNR poorly specifies the relationship between the various criminogenic needs and their theoretical grounding. This is because the RNR model is a rehabilitation theory and not an etiological theory of a *particular type* of offending. It is a *framework theory* and is meant to guide therapists and correctional workers in the rehabilitation process. It relies on more local theories of particular crimes to supplement its general explanation of crime, and without these it will appear to be rather impoverished in terms of explanatory power. Unfortunately, it is not always clear from the literature on the RNR model that its etiological assumptions are meant to be only very general in nature and should not be viewed as adequate explanations of crime (i.e. the assumptions derived from GPSPP and PIC-R). In our view, the confusion has arisen from a failure to distinguish between etiological, practice and rehabilitation theories. Therefore, researchers and clinicians have sometimes erroneously thought of PCC, GPSPP and PIC-R as explanatory theories that ground the practice implications of the three principles of risk, need and responsivity. We consider this to be a mistake and that instead the aim should be explicitly to construct rehabilitation theories with etiological components.

PRACTICE IMPLICATIONS

The applied aspect of RNR is both its strongest component and also in many respects its weakest. While there is an impressive range of support for the three key principles of RNR, there are also some major limitations. These are in part due to the problems noted above in the first two components: restricted range of values and conceptualization of risk, and vague and overly diffuse etiological assumptions.

A major strength is the fact that a strong empirical base underpins the theory, so assessment and treatment strategies are carefully evaluated and tested to ensure their validity and reliability (McGuire, 2002). There is accumulating research evidence for the three principles underlying treatment indicating that lowered recidivism rates are a direct result of treating higher-risk offenders more intensively, targeting criminogenic needs, and matching treatment to the particular features of offenders such as learning style and motivation, etc. (e.g. Andrews and Bonta, 2003; Andrews and Dowden, 2006; Dowden and Andrews, 2003; Lipsey, 1992; Lösel, 1995; Lowenkamp, Latessa and Holsinger, 2006). This particular strength underlines the *empirical adequacy* and practical utility (*fertility*) of the RNR model.

Risk principle. The risk principle suggests that offenders assessed as being at high risk for offending should receive higher levels of intervention, including high-intensity treatment. Many empirical studies have provided support for the risk principle (e.g. Andrews and Dowden, 2006; Lowenkamp, Latessa and Holsinger, 2006) but perhaps the most comprehensive of these is Andrews and Dowden's (2006) meta-analysis. Of course, how risk is measured has a marked effect on the level of empirical support for the risk principle. Andrews and Dowden examined studies that differentiated between risk levels *within* their samples (i.e. divide their sample into two or more groups based on level of risk). They found that only 44 out of 374 available comparisons differentiated their samples according to this method. For the other 330 comparisons, the established *aggregate* approach was applied. Within this approach, whether or not the majority of the sample had prior convictions was used as the measure of risk. Andrews and Dowden (2006), suggest that reliance on the aggregate method has resulted in a dampening of the risk effect in the empirical analyses conducted thus far, since there is a stronger relationship between effect size and risk in studies using a within-sample differentiation of risk than in those for whom the aggregate approach is used. Thus, empirical support for the risk principle may be somewhat diluted, as a result of the coding strategies utilized.

In research utilizing the aggregate approach, support for the risk principle has been moderate. Andrews and Dowden (2006) found that studies using high-risk participants had mean effect sizes of $r = 0.10$ compared to $r = 0.03$ for those that targeted lower-risk clients (according to Cohen, 1988, an effect size of $r = .10$ is small, $r = .30$ is medium, and $r = .50$ is large). Interestingly, support for the risk principle has been greater among juvenile than among adult offenders. Andrews and Dowden (2006) report that the benefit of targeting high- as opposed to low-risk offenders is much greater for juveniles (in high-risk samples $r = 0.26$ versus $r = 0.07$ in low-risk samples) than for adults (high-risk samples provide $r = 0.15$ versus low-risk $r = 0.13$). These positive findings dovetail with other reports of juvenile delinquents benefiting from the application of the risk principle. For example, in a sample of juvenile offender comparisons, treatments that targeted groups of delinquents with a high proportion of prior offenses were more effective than those that did not (mean effect sizes of 0.12 and 0.03 respectively; Dowden and Andrews, 1999a). Lipsey (1992) reported similar findings, although the effect was small and non-significant. In a sample of 200 studies targeting serious juvenile delinquents, treatment effects were larger for more serious offense types and in studies where all (as opposed to most) delinquents had prior offenses (Lipsey and Wilson, 2002). Similarly, Latimer (2001) concludes that treatment may be more effective for repeat offenders. Clearly, the risk principle is strongly supported in research on juveniles. This raises the question of why empirical support for the principle remains so limited in the adult offender population. This difference may in part be due to an interaction between age and the aggregate coding method. The aggregate coding method may be less appropriate for adults since a greater proportion will already have prior offenses (Andrews and Dowden, 2006).

Need principle. The need principle proposes that only variables empirically associated with offending reduction should be targeted in treatment. The need principle is based on a subset of risk factors – dynamic risk factors or criminogenic needs (Bonta, 2002; Bonta and Andrews, 2003). In the meta-analyses of Andrews, Dowden and colleagues, adherence to the need principle is generally coded according to whether or not there were more criminogenic needs targeted than noncriminogenic needs (e.g. Dowden and Andrews, 1999a; Andrews and Bonta, 2003). Note that this operationalization of the need principle does not provide any indication of the adequacy of the treatment or the amount of time spent on the needs, simply that they were targeted in greater numbers than were noncriminogenic needs. It also has the bizarre effect of penalizing a program for helping meet individuals' noncriminogenic needs. So, for instance, a program that targets three criminogenic needs and one non-criminogenic need will have a "good" score, but if the same program were also to raise individuals' self-esteem, help them with financial problems, provide counseling for depression and give them an opportunity to express their artistic abilities (noncriminogenic needs, all) the program would receive a "negative" ratio simply because it met so many other needs.

Still, there has been strong empirical support for the need principle. In Andrews and Bonta's (2003) updated meta-analysis of general offender populations (including 374 comparisons) they find that programs targeting a greater number of criminogenic needs than noncrimino-genic needs have mean effect sizes of $r = 0.19$ compared with $r = -0.01$ if they do not target criminogenic needs. The positive effects of adherence to the need principle have been found in a variety of offender populations, including female offenders (Dowden and Andrews, 1999b) and juvenile offenders (Dowden and Andrews, 1999a).

Other findings of note regarding the need principle relate to the greater gains evident when treatments adhere to certain program features (PF) noted earlier (e.g. manual-based, utilizing behavioral interventions, etc.) or are targeted at higher-risk cases. First, when at least one feature of PF is present, the gains from adherence to the need principle are greater than when no PF components are present (increases from $r = -0.04$ to $r = 0.24$ versus $r = 0.07$ to $r = 0.15$ respectively; Dowden and Andrews, 2004). Thus, the provision of PF may provide the context within which the need principle is most effective, suggesting that the RNR model is clearly a higher-order model that requires effective treatment practices in order to be effective.

As well as focusing on the need principle, Andrews, Dowden and colleagues have provided some detailed examinations of the effectiveness of treatments that target specific criminogenic needs. Andrews and Bonta's (2003) updated meta-analysis of 374 general offender comparisons provides support for the efficacy of targeting a number of personal criminogenic needs, including antisocial cognitions, self-control deficits, and school or work interventions. Interestingly, programs targeting substance abuse did not result in significantly greater treatment effects. Furthermore, focusing on modifying noncriminogenic needs such as fear of official punishment, personal distress, or family processing (other than nurturance, supervision) did not result in reduced recidivism.

Responsivity principle. In contrast to the voluminous research on general responsivity, and despite numerous calls for its closer examination (e.g. Andrews *et al.*, 2006), the effects of specific responsivity on treatment outcome remain relatively unexplored (Bonta, 1995). This has largely been due to the difficulty in coding specific responsivity in meta-analyses.

General responsivity describes the role of treatment-level issues in the match between treatment modality and offenders' learning style. For example, cognitive-behavioral strategies are considered to be the best way to change offenders' problematic behavior (Andrews and Bonta, 2003). *Specific responsivity* refers to the individual characteristics of offenders which will make them more or less likely to engage with treatment.

In Andrews, Dowden and colleagues' meta-analyses, the coding of data related to general responsivity is based on whether or not the program was based on social learning or cognitive-behavioral theory and used role-playing, reinforcement and graduated practice (e.g. Dowden and Andrews, 1999a, 1999b, 2003). In Andrews and Bonta's (2003) updated meta-analysis of the effectiveness of correctional treatment for general offender groups, studies that met this criterion had larger effects than studies that did not (mean $r = 0.23$, compared to 0.04). The same results have been found in samples of juvenile delinquents (mean $r = 0.24$, compared to 0.04), female offenders (mean $r = 0.27$, compared to 0.08) and violent offenders (mean $r = 0.19$, compared to 0.01; Dowden and Andrews, 1999a, 1999b, 2000). These findings are consistent with a robust literature suggesting that cognitive-behavioral programs are the most effective treatment modality in reducing recidivism across a wide variety of offender groups (e.g. Pearson, Lipton, Cleland and Yee, 2002; Lipsey, Chapman and Landenberger, 2001; Hanson *et al.*, 2002; Salekin, 2002; Redondo, Sanchez-Meca and Garrido, 2002).

It is important to note that general responsivity does not affect offender responsivity in isolation. Rather, general factors in combination with specific offender characteristics may impede or facilitate offenders' readiness to change (Serin and Kennedy, 1997). In other words, responsivity is concerned with how the individual interacts with the treatment environment, and covers a range of factors and situations (see Ward, Polaschek and Beech, 2006). Research suggests that staff characteristics such as warmth, humor and expressions of empathy, and appropriate modelling and reinforcement may also be critical to treatment outcome (Dowden and Andrews, 2004; Marshall and Serran, 2004). The finding that responsivity is affected by a wide range of external and internal factors is not surprising and points to the need to examine further the responsivity construct and its role in correctional intervention.

Conflicting outcome data. The empirical support for the RNR model is impressive and certainly suggests that offenders treated according to its major principles are more likely to desist from committing further offenses. However, alongside these triumphs there have been failures where the delivery of criminogenic programs has not worked well and in some cases has been discontinued.

One example is the implementation of reasoning and rehabilitation (R&R). R&R is a multifaceted program designed to teach offenders social cognitive skills and values associated with "prosocial social competence" (Antonowicz, 2005, p. 163). For RNR advocates, R&R is a perfect example of "what works" – a systematic, manual-based program that targets the right criminogenic needs in measured doses. The core cognitive skills imparted in R&R have been shown to modify effectively a number of problems associated with offending including impulsivity, externality, concrete thinking, conceptual rigidity, impaired interpersonal problem-solving, egocentricity, inappropriate values, and poor critical reasoning (e.g. Ross, 1995; Ross, Antonowicz and Dhaliwal, 1995; Ross and Fabiano, 1983).

R&R programs have been the subject of a series of important reviews recently, and the evidence is decidedly mixed. In one, Antonowicz (2005) found that overall R&R programs are effective in leading to reduced reoffending rates, although there have been some disappointing outcomes, in particular in a number of high-profile and costly experiments in the United Kingdom (see Cann *et al.*, 2003; Falshaw *et al.*, 2003; Lewis *et al.*, 2003). Antonowicz (2005) identifies plausible reasons for these and other occasional R&R treatment failures such as poor treatment integrity, the need for booster sessions, inattention to responsivity issues, and so on. Wilson and colleagues (2005) also found very mixed outcomes for structured cognitive rehabilitation programs, with a mean overall effect size of 0.16 (see also Lipsey *et al.*, 2001).

In another recent review of R&R programs Tong and Farrington (2006) conducted a meta-analysis involving thirty-eight treatment and control effect-size comparisons. In this study the effect size was measured using Odds Ratio (OR), and outcomes included reconviction/rearrest, revocation/technical violation, and return to prison. Only five of the independent odds ratio comparisons showed statistically significant differences in favor of the treatment group having a better outcome than the control group. These five positive findings came from four independent evaluations. Several of the comparisons produced ORs less than 1 (which indicated that the treatment group fared worse than the control group) but these comparisons did not reach statistical significance. The meta-analysis found R&R was more effective in the community than in institutions, which is consistent with general findings in offender rehabilitation. More problematically, Tong and Farrington (2006) found that R&R was more effective with low-risk offenders compared to high-risk offenders. Although this difference did not reach significance, it appears to contradict the central RNR risk principle in which higher-risk offenders are assumed to benefit more from treatment than low-risk offenders. Tong and Farrington made a couple of notable criticisms of the R&R treatment program, namely that (*a*) it individualizes criminality without taking into account social and economic contexts/influences that are known to associate with crime rates and that (*b*) program integrity and implementation issues are too easy a default explanation for poor outcomes. They argue that, to assess this fairly, program integrity should be measured before outcomes are known (see also Lin, 2000; Logan and Gaes, 1993; Mair, 2004). Indeed, the frequent pointing to "implementation" to explain any negative findings leads to the question of whether implementation can ever be blamed when "things go right"? That is, if implementation issues are so crucial to outcomes, it should be equally possible that these factors (staff dedication, program social climate, warmth, sense of humor, client group fit, and culture) – and not the program's model or targeting of risks – account for rehabilitative success.

The fact that the evidence for R&R and other criminogenic needs programs has not always been positive does not mean that they are necessarily weak or poor interventions. Relatedly, the findings do not refute RNR as a whole. Rather, the existence of failures points to the challenges and complexities of correctional treatment and reminds us to continue thinking about ways to improve what we offer offenders. In our view, some of the difficulties noted in the delivery of RNR-type programs have their origins in the kinds of problem outlined below. In other words, it is possible that the RNR model does not have the conceptual and practical resources to provide a comprehensive guide for working therapeutically with offenders. The explicit targeting of risk may be a necessary but not sufficient condition for reducing reoffending.

Risk and treatment. This point concerns the clinical utility of using estimated risk levels to make decisions about the type and extent of treatment offenders receive. As reviewed above, there is empirical evidence supporting this procedure, but the practice remains problematic for several normative and pragmatic reasons. On a normative level, intervening in human lives requires consideration of human welfare issues as well as recidivism issues. On a pragmatic level, though, individuals are much more likely to respond to treatment initiatives if they feel therapists are genuinely interested in them as people and also if they expect to have a better life as a consequence of the intervention (e.g. see Bottoms, 2000; Kelman, 1958).

Individuals who are assessed as low-risk may exhibit a number of significant problems that adversely impact on their functioning, such as low mood or relationship conflict. Although such problems may not be criminogenic needs, individuals could still benefit from therapeutic attention, and the untreated problems may have a downstream effect on their chances of being effectively rehabilitated. For instance, a person who is feeling depressed or anxious may fail to apply for a potentially valuable vocational program because he sees it as irrelevant to his current problems. It is also possible that the psychological consequences of not being treated for noncriminogenic needs could later result in increased offending and subsequent elevated risk level. For example, feelings of resentment and deprivation arising from refusal of one's right to treatment could lead to aggressive behavior in prison and development of antisocial tendencies. It is important to note that this point is based on clinical observation and not currently supported by research evidence, which appears to demonstrate the irrelevance of targeting noncriminogenic needs.

Another issue is that it is possible to encounter offenders who are assessed as high-risk but appear to have relatively low needs, at least in some respects. Such individuals could have quite circumscribed problems that may put them at risk for reoffending, but do not display a *wide range* of problems. For example, a high-functioning sexual offender may have specific problems in establishing intimate relationships with adults but possess excellent self-regulation, emotional and general social skills (Ward and Siegert, 2002). Such an individual might need intensive therapeutic work to modify his deeply rooted fears about intimacy but very little else. The danger is that by designating him as high-risk the assumption will be that he also has significant clinical needs, and he may be subjected to hours of needless, non-targeted therapy. What this example illustrates is the dependence of the risk principle on a comprehensive measure of criminogenic needs that allows for a determination of the number and severity of a person's problems and their causal relationship to his offense. An alternative would be to transcend simple psychometric assessment and instead endorse the explicit construction of a case formulation (McGuire, 2000). An explicit case formulation in essence represents a clinical theory of an offender's stable dynamic risk factors, their relationships, and the likelihood of these being activated in particular situations. Thus, the relationship between level of risk (an estimate or prediction) and level of clinical need is a complex one and not exhausted by the symmetry implied in the risk–need principle (i.e. high risk equates to greater number of needs).

Criminogenic needs as range riders. Criminogenic needs are for the most part little more than range riders – they simply inform therapists that a problem exists in some domain but do not specify how it is to be resolved. For this, substantive theories about the need in question (for example, impulsiveness or deviant sexual preferences) are required. Such a theory should spell out how to effect change in the relevant mechanisms that cause impulsiveness and also explain how it relates to other criminogenic needs. It should also explain how the particular criminogenic need in question is generated and what mechanisms are currently contributing to its maintenance. This is clinically useful because different etiological pathways to offending require distinct intervention plans. A policy that simply states that criminogenic needs should be primary treatment targets without invoking additional theory and clinical models will not result in effective treatment.

Motivational issues. Focusing on risk reduction in treatment is unlikely to motivate offenders to make the major changes required to reduce their chances of reoffending (see Fabiano and Porporino, 2002). Motivation involves two types of goal: avoidance and approach goals (Austin and Vancouver, 1996). *Avoidance goals* are concerned with the modification, reduction or elimination of experiences, states of affairs and characteristics, while *approach goals* are concerned with the realization of these factors. Ruth Mann and colleagues have recently demonstrated that it is easier to motivate offenders by focusing on approach goals (i.e. promoting goods or personally endorsed adaptive goals) rather than on avoidance goals (i.e. stopping offending) in therapy (Mann, Webster, Schofield and Marshall, 2004). Likewise, in the addiction recovery literature, Amodeo, Kurtz and Cutter (1992, p. 709) speculate that "negative" or "avoidant" motives, such as fear of arrest, physical deterioration, family breakup or job loss, might be the most common incentives for "putting down the bottle", yet more positive or "approach" motives such as a sense of purpose in life or a commitment to occupational success might be the more influential force in maintaining sobriety. Avoidant motives can be powerful catalysts for action, they suggest, but they may not be able to sustain long-term resolve against powerful temptations (see also Braithwaite and Roche, 2001, and their discussion of "passive responsibility" versus "active responsibility").

In general, the evidence from research on motivation supports the utility of emphasizing approach goals when seeking to induce behavior change rather than concentrating solely on reducing, eliminating or modifying problematic behaviors (see McMurran and Ward, 2004). Focusing *only* on the reduction of criminogenic needs may reduce risk, but without inculcating other methods to achieve goals risk is likely to reemerge (Duguid, 2000). Importantly, a focus on promoting strengths or approach goals is not inconsistent with the overarching aims of the RNR model; it is simply an underdeveloped aspect of the model.

Importance of noncriminogenic needs. An additional criticism revolves around the RNR model's distinction between criminogenic and noncriminogenic needs. Although this distinction is empirically correct (that is, some measures of needs appear statistically related to offending whereas others are not), making this distinction in a therapeutic relationship makes less sense (indeed, might even be impossible in some cases). Targeting noncriminogenic needs might often be a necessary condition of targeting criminogenic needs by virtue of the fact that any intervention requires that offenders are sufficiently attentive and receptive to the therapeutic content of sessions (Ward and Stewart, 2003). Personal distress, financial crises, low self-esteem, and interpersonal distrust (all noncriminogenic needs) can impact on the development of the therapeutic alliance and make it difficult for the therapist to deliver standard RNR model interventions. As a matter of course, therapists should direct attention to some types of noncriminogenic needs, not just because it is ethical and "good" to do so, but because of the value this has on sustaining a sound therapeutic alliance. Research by Marshall, Serran and colleagues (2003) has demonstrated that the establishment of a strong therapeutic alliance is necessary for effective interventions even though such work is not directly concerned with targeting risk. In other words, attending to features of individuals' lives such as personal distress or the interpersonal manifestations of low self-esteem is a mandatory not a discretionary aspect of effective therapy.

Again, this is really a problem of omission rather than of commission for the RNR model. There is nothing inherent to RNR principles that precludes attending to noncriminogenic needs. It is simply not adequately addressed.

"One size fits all". Rightly or wrongly, the RNR model is often translated in practice into a "one size fits all" policy that fails to take critical individual needs and values into account. Despite the emphasis on responsivity intrinsic to the model, the implementation of RNR in correctional settings typically involves a mechanistic, workbook-based approach to groupwork with prisoners or probationers. Offenders are screened for risk level and criminogenic needs, and then allocated to varying dosages of "cog skills" workshops according to their assessment results. The point as to the problem with a focus on "programs" rather than on "people" has been made by numerous critics of RNR (see Mair, 2004). These programs are selected on the basis of their demonstrated ability to ameliorate dynamic risk factors and are typically manualized and delivered in a group format.

Of course, generic programs like these may fail to address important preferences and circumstances pertaining to individual offenders. Human beings are embedded in local social and cultural contexts, so any treatment plan should focus on the skills and resources required to function in the particular contexts they are likely to be released into (Ward and Stewart 2003). The trouble with most manual-based programs is that they tend to have built into them generic conceptions concerning what kinds of goods or goals should be achieved rather than taking into account individual offenders' capabilities, preferences and likely living circumstances. This requires an awareness of both their goals and the environment into which they are likely to be released. Factors such as opportunities, resources and social identities constrain what is possible to achieve and should be factored into any therapeutic program. Unfortunately, the RNR model is not equipped to allow for such adjustments easily because of its focus on risk factors rather than on whole persons who live in complex communities.

The fact that the RNR model is usually unpacked in terms of the three principles means that it is relatively easy to neglect the etiological and overarching principles and aims that are essential parts of it. Thus, the practice elements have been insulated from the more theoretical components, helped by the loose and rather unsystematic way the RNR model has been formulated in the past. As such, the model lacks ecological validity and in this respect suffers from lack of explanatory depth and also therapeutic fertility.

CONCLUSIONS: EVALUATING RNR

So how does the RNR model measure up as a correctional rehabilitation theory? From our critical examination it is apparent that this influential theory contains a fair number of strengths and also some weaknesses. The fact that treatment targets and interventions are empirically derived means that outcomes are likely to be positive. Furthermore, the utilization of structured assessment and structured treatment strategies is also a useful feature of the practice aspects of this rehabilitation theory. In short, the RNR model of offender rehabilitation represents a significant achievement. Its application by correctional services throughout the world has resulted in reduced recidivism rates and safer communities. The requirement that treatment should ensure that dynamic risk factors are eliminated, reduced or managed is sensible and likely to resonate with policy-makers and the general public alike.

However, despite its many virtues, the model can be criticized because of what are perceived as theoretical, policy and practice weaknesses. We have argued that one of the major reasons for these problems resides in the way the RNR model has been developed and applied. Essentially, the primary emphasis has been on the practical utility of the three major principles of risk, need and responsivity, and therefore the theoretical underpinnings of the model (i.e. how should it work) have been underdeveloped. In fact, the three models that have been used to justify or ground the assumptions of the RNR model have been insufficiently integrated with the practice components. In order to remedy this difficulty we have reconstructed the RNR model using a three-level structure: overall aims, principles and values; etiological and methodological assumptions; and practice implications. The result is a more integrated, systematic theory of rehabilitation that is better able to guide therapists.

However, even in its stronger form the RNR still suffers from a lack of theoretical depth and thus does not help correctional workers adequately engage in a number of important intervention tasks. The narrowness of its basic assumptions and value commitments means that the primary etiological elements of RNR revolve around the detection and role of risk factors in the generation of crime. The failure of RNR explicitly to consider a broader range of human needs and the role of identity and agency in offending means that it ultimately pays insufficient attention to core therapeutic and intervention tasks (e.g. treatment alliance, motivational issues). Thus, there is a cascading effect sweeping down from the level of basic assumptions, through etiological foci, and culminating in an overemphasis on risk-management practice.

The limitations of RNR elaborated above signal the desirability of making changes in the way correctional interventions are designed and implemented. One possible change might be to pay more attention to therapist and process variables, and seek to establish a sound therapeutic relationship prior to employing the technical aspects of therapy (Horvath and Luborsky, 1993). Second, it is also important to understand the problematic internal and external conditions that are associated with, or in fact constitute, the offender's criminogenic needs, and to build interventions around the amelioration of these problematic conditions. It is helpful to view criminogenic needs as red flags that signal a problem in the way offenders are seeking important personal goals. Third, ensuring that an intervention plan based on criminogenic needs is presented to offenders in the form of both approach and avoidant goals rather than exclusively in terms of risk management could enhance treatment motivations and outcome.

In other words, what is needed is a rehabilitation theory that incorporates the strengths of RNR while increasing its scope and capacity to guide correctional workers and engage offenders in the demanding process of lifestyle change. This means incorporating significant parts of the RNR model within a broader rehabilitation theory. To this end, in the next two chapters we focus on describing and critically appraising the Good Lives Model of offender rehabilitation.

5

THE GOOD LIVES MODEL OF OFFENDER REHABILITATION

In this chapter we describe Ward and colleagues' Good Lives Model (GLM) of rehabilitation, a "strengths-based" approach (see Maruna and LeBel, 2003) to the treatment of individuals in the criminal justice system. The Good Lives Model (Ward and Brown, 2004; Ward and Marshall, 2004) was formulated as an alternative approach to correctional treatment that has the conceptual resources to integrate aspects of treatment not well dealt with by the RNR perspective, such as the formation of a therapeutic alliance and motivating individuals to engage in the difficult process of changing their life. The GLM has been most extensively applied to rehabilitation work with sex offenders, and therefore the assessment process and interventions with this population have been developed in the most detail. However, the GLM was designed to apply to all types of criminal behavior and it has recently been used effectively in working with individuals convicted of violent non-sex-related crimes (see Whitehead, Ward and Collie, in press).

With the GLM we propose that there is a direct relationship between goods promotion and risk management in rehabilitation work. In brief, we argue that a focus on the promotion of specific goods or goals is likely automatically to eliminate or modify commonly targeted dynamic risk factors (i.e. criminogenic needs). That is, assisting individuals to achieve goods via non-offending methods may function to eliminate or reduce the need for offending.

There are three strands to our argument. First, we propose that the pursuit of primary human goods is implicated in the etiology of offending. By virtue of possessing the same needs and nature as the rest of us, offenders actively search for primary human goods in their environment (e.g. relationships, mastery experiences, a sense of belonging, a sense of purpose, and autonomy). In some circumstances (e.g. through lack of internal skills and external conditions), this can lead to antisocial behavior. Second, we argue that therapeutic actions that promote approach goals will also help to secure avoidance goals. This occurs because of the etiological role that goods play in offending, and also because equipping individuals with the internal and external conditions necessary effectively to implement a good life plan (i.e. a plan that contains all the primary goods and ways of achieving them that match the individuals' abilities, preferences and environment) will also modify their criminogenic needs. Third, it is easier to motivate individuals to change their offense-related characteristics by focusing on the perceived benefits (primary goods) they accrue from their offending and by exploring more appropriate means (secondary goods) to achieve what is of value to them. By proceeding in this manner, individuals do not need to abandon those things that are important to them – only to learn to acquire them differently.

POSITIVE PSYCHOLOGY AND THE GOOD LIFE

The notion of the "good life" has occupied philosophers for centuries, but has only recently become the subject of empirical psychology (see King, Eells and Burton, 2004; Peterson and Seligman, 2004; Seligman, 2002). Psychologists have traditionally focused either on mental health (i.e. the absence of mental illness) or else on related constructs like "happiness" (Diener *et al.*, 1999) or "self-esteem" (Rosenberg, 1965). King and her colleagues (2004) recently investigated "folk notions" of the good life among lay persons (both student and community samples) and found that members of the public largely saw the good life as involving two distinct dimensions: personal happiness and finding meaning in life. This distinction between *eudaimonic* (i.e. growth-based, purposeful) and *hedonic* (i.e. pleasure-based) aspects of the good life has an impressive pedigree behind it dating back at least to Aristotle, who argued that the good life combined both pleasure and virtue.

Positive psychology has emerged out of this ancient Greek view that human beings are naturally oriented toward seeking personal fulfillment (i.e. the achievement of excellence) and, furthermore, that a flourishing life is only possible if these potentialities are realized (Jorgensen and Nafstad, 2004; Peterson and Seligman, 2004). Positive psychology focuses on promoting human welfare and individual strengths rather than on emphasizing and hence potentially exacerbating psychosocial deficits (Aspinwall and Staudinger, 2003). It is a strengths-based approach in that it seeks to equip people with the capabilities to meet their needs, pursue their interests, and therefore live happy, fulfilling lives.

This sense of fulfillment is not to be confused with the *hedonic* state of pleasure but rather refers to a deeply satisfying lifestyle that extends over a number of domains and a significant period of time. Thus, a person could be happy in the sense that he or she tends to experience pleasant states but be essentially unfulfilled. In other words, such individuals are choosing to live in ways that deny important aspects of their character and needs; they are not striving to realize their potential as human beings. For example, a person could squander his or her talents in pleasure-seeking and neglect his or her needs for personal meaning, autonomy, relatedness, mastery and creativity. According to this perspective on human functioning, individuals' sense of identity emerges from their basic value commitments, the goods they pursue in search of a better life. The bridge between goods and meaning is well described by Archer (2000, p. 10), who states that:

> In short, we are who we are because of what we care about: in delineating our ultimate concerns and accommodating our subordinate ones, we also define ourselves. We give a shape to our lives, which constitutes our internal personal integrity.

The idea of human flourishing has persisted throughout history and has clearly influenced researchers over the centuries to think beyond simple harm-avoidance and pleasure-seeking when it comes to understanding and designing ways of modifying human behavior. In fact it is possible to trace the Greek view of happiness or well-being through a line of philosophers, researchers, scholars and psychologists from the Middle Ages and the Enlightenment to modern theorists such as Werner, Maslow, Lewin, Rogers, MacIntyre, Seligman and Csikszentmihalyi (Jorgensen and Nafstad, 2004). The emphasis on attending to human nature and personal fulfillment indicates the strong humanistic strand in positive psychology.

EXPLAINING THE GOOD LIVES MODEL

The GLM is an example of a positive-psychology or strengths-based approach to rehabilitation, although it was developed independently of the positive psychology movement. The aim of positive treatment approaches to psychological and behavioral problems is to enhance individuals' capacity to live meaningful, constructive and ultimately happy lives so that they can desist from further criminal actions and/or become symptom-free. One of the key assumptions of positive psychological theories is that all human beings are naturally inclined to seek certain types of experience or human good, and that they experience high levels of well-being if these goods are obtained. Criminal actions are thought to arise when individuals lack the internal and external resources to attain their goals in pro-social ways. In other words, crime and psychological problems are hypothesized to be a direct consequence of maladaptive attempts to meet human needs (Ward and Stewart, 2003). From the perspective of positive psychology, in order for individuals to desist from offending they should be given the knowledge, skills, opportunities and resources to live a "good" life, which takes into account their particular preferences, interests and values. In short, treatment should provide them with a chance to be better people with better lives.

The GLM thus provides a framework for intervening therapeutically with individuals of all types. There are three levels or components to the GLM (see Figure 5.1): (a) a set of general principles and assumptions that specify the values that underlie rehabilitation practice and the kind of overall aims that clinicians should be striving for; (b) etiological assumptions that serve to explain offending and identify its functions, at least in a general sense; and (c) the intervention implications of both the set of values, aims and principles, and the etiological assumptions. We shall now briefly discuss each of these components in turn.

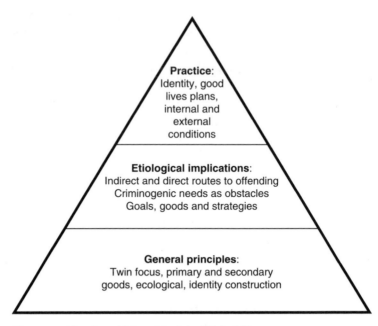

Figure 5.1 The Good Lives Model of Rehabilitation

PRINCIPLES, AIMS AND VALUES OF THE GLM

First, the GLM assumes that, because of their status as human beings, offenders share the same inclinations and basic needs as other people and are naturally predisposed to seek certain goals, or *primary human goods* (e.g. relatedness, creativity, physical health, and mastery). According to the GLM, these primary goods have their source in human nature and have evolved through natural selection to help people establish strong social networks and to survive and reproduce. Arnhart (1998, p. 29) labels these goods "natural desires" because "they are so deeply rooted in human nature that they will manifest themselves in some manner across history in every human society". Primary human goods are linked to certain ways of living that, if pursued, involve the actualization of potentialities that are distinctively human. These goods all contribute to a happy or fulfilling life but are intrinsically valuable in themselves.

In essence, *primary* goods are states of affairs, states of mind, personal characteristics, activities or experiences that are sought for their own sake and are likely to increase psychological well-being if achieved (Kekes, 1989; Ward and Stewart, 2003). That is, they have intrinsic value and represent the fundamental purposes and ultimate ends of human behavior. The psychological, social, biological and anthropological research evidence provides support for the existence of at least ten groups of primary human goods (see Aspinwall and Staudinger, 2003; Cummins, 1996; Deci and Ryan, 2000; Emmons, 1999; Linley and Joseph, 2004; Murphy, 2001; Nussbaum, 2000), including:

- Life (including healthy living and physical functioning)
- Knowledge
- Excellence in play and work (including mastery experiences)
- Agency (i.e. autonomy and self-directedness)
- Inner peace (i.e. freedom from emotional turmoil and stress)
- Friendship (including intimate, romantic and family relationships)
- Community
- Spirituality (in the broad sense of finding meaning and purpose in life)
- Happiness
- Creativity

Although this list is extensive, it is not meant to be exhaustive, and we are not wedded to the list of goods outlined above. However, we argue that the available research indicates that the goods listed are likely to appear in some form on any list generated (Aspinwall and Staudinger, 2003; Cummins, 1996; Emmons, 1999, 2003; Nussbaum, 2000; Ward and Stewart, 2003). It is also possible to subdivide the primary goods noted above into subgroups. For example, the good of relatedness could be further divided into goods such as the provision and experience of mutual support, sexual activity, personal disclosure, physical comfort and emotional reassurance.

In addition to these primary goods, *instrumental* or secondary goods provide particular ways (i.e. means) of achieving primary goods, for example, certain types of work or relationship. For instance, it is possible to secure the primary good of relatedness via romantic, parental or personal relationships among other means. The notion of instrumental goods or means is particularly important when it comes to applying the GLM to offending behavior as it is assumed that a primary reason individuals commit offenses is the pursuit of more abstract primary goods albeit in destructive and ultimately unsatisfying ways (see the section on etiology below).

The GLM has a relatively robust conception of human nature that differs from that of evolutionary psychology. According to evolutionary psychologists, over millions of years natural selection has molded the brain into a multipurpose instrument that enables organisms to survive and reproduce in a hostile environment world (Tooby and Cosmides, 1992). Theorists advocating the narrow evolutionary psychology perspective assert that human beings are born with a dense or "thick" structure and a rich suite of psychological competencies. Human nature is hypothesized to unfold inexorably in certain types of environment and in a significant sense is *preformed* by the workings of evolutionary forces (Buller and Hardcastle, 2000).

By way of contrast, we agree with gene-culture co-evolution theorists that human beings have a considerable degree of psychological plasticity and are significantly shaped by their environment (Odling-Smee, Laland and Feldman, 2003). According to Andy Clark (2003), brains are scaffolded from the moment of birth by an impressive suite of learning opportunities and deliberately engineered environments that allow each person to construct a self as well as the skills and competencies to pursue his or her vision of a good life. Individuals are born into a world replete with a number of different developmental resources ranging from one's culture, subculture, family unit, genetically encoded predispositions, role models and learning experiences. These resources equally influence human development and are all important in the process of facilitating their growth from birth to maturity. In a nutshell, humans are co-constructed through the delicate interplay between biological, psychological, social and environmental variables (Tomasello, 1999).

An especially significant characteristic of the GLM is that the goods are plural rather than singular, and therefore a fulfilling life will most probably require access to all the primary goods even though individuals can legitimately vary in the way they value or rank them. This means that there are multiple sources of motivation and that each has its origin in the evolved nature of human beings. It is also important to emphasize that the goods referred to in the GLM model are *prudential* rather than moral or epistemic goods. That is, they are experiences and activities that are likely to result in enhanced levels of well-being rather than morally good actions or features of good theories. There is no assumption in the GLM that individuals are inherently or naturally good in an ethical sense. Rather, the presumption is that, because of their nature, human beings are more likely to function well if they have access to the various types of good outlined above.

A second major assumption of the GLM is that rehabilitation is a value-laden process and involves a variety of different types of value including prudential values (what is in the best interests of individual clients), ethical values (what is in the best interests of community), and epistemic or knowledge-related values (what are our best-practice models and methods). The construction of a more adaptive narrative identity involves orienting individuals to the range of primary goods, helping them understand how the pursuit of these legitimate goals led them to illegal behaviors, and providing them with the resources to secure better lives in ways that are personally satisfying and socially acceptable. Prudential goods provide the fundamental goals toward which individuals strive. Epistemic goods are utilized to devise methods of achieving them that are reliable and responsive to the environments in which they are embedded. Thus, values and facts are inextricably linked.

A third assumption is closely related to the first two and states that correctional interventions should aim both to (a) promote individuals' relevant goods as well as (b) manage/reduce risk. In addition, it is assumed that, because criminogenic needs and human needs are causally related (see below), the promotion of adaptive approach goals should also reduce dynamic risk factors. Thus, a major aim of correctional reintegration work is to help individuals to construct a life plan that has the basic primary goods, and ways of effectively securing them, built into it and does not involve inflicting harm on others. According to the GLM, risk factors represent omissions or distortions in the internal and external conditions required to implement a good lives plan in a specific set of environments. Installing the internal conditions (i.e. skills, values, beliefs) and the external conditions (resources, social supports, opportunities) is likely to reduce or eliminate each individual's set of criminogenic needs.

A fourth major assumption is that the process of rehabilitation requires not just the targeting of isolated "factors", but also the holistic reconstruction of the "self". The GLM emphasizes the overarching construct of personal identity and its relationship to individuals' understanding of what constitutes a good life. According to theory and research on identity development and personal strivings, individuals' self-conceptions directly arise from their basic value commitments and the way in which they are expressed in their daily activities (Deci and Ryan, 2000; Emmons, 1999; Singer, 2005). In other words, people acquire a sense of who they are and what really matters from what they do. What this means for correctional practitioners is that it is not enough simply to equip individuals with skills to control or reduce their risk factors; it is essential that they are also given the opportunity to acquire a more adaptive personal identity, one that gives them a sense of meaning and fulfillment.

A fifth assumption is that human beings are multifaceted beings comprised of a variety of interconnected biological, social, cultural and psychological systems, and are interdependent to a significant degree. What this means is that complex animals such as human beings can only flourish within a community that provides emotional support, material resources, education, and even the means of survival. The complexity of human functioning means that an adequate explanation of something as important as crime will require multiple levels of analysis and theoretical perspectives. In particular, the interdependency of human behavior points to the necessity of adopting an ecological framework. This is because of people's reliance on other life forms and cultural resources. According to Steiner (2002, p. 2), "Ecology is, by definition, the reciprocal relationship among all organisms and their biological and physical environments. People are organisms." In our view, thinking of the cultural, social and personal circumstances as ecological components helps to keep in mind the fact that human beings are animals who purposively interact with their environment and develop in a dynamic and interactive manner. Therefore, offending emerges from a network of relationships between individuals and their local environments, and is not simply the consequence of individual psychopathology.

The fact that human beings are interdependent and that, therefore, a satisfactory understanding of behavior will always involve an appreciation of the contexts in which they exist has important implications for therapists when designing reintegration programs. Thus, according to the GLM, any assessment and intervention should take into account the match between the *characteristics* of the individual and the likely *environment* he or she will be released into. In other words, we assert that when seeking to promote adaptive functioning it is necessary to grasp the specific contexts in which individuals live and the unique challenges they face. The idea of context-free intervention, then, is clearly a mistake.

Sixth, because people are conceptualized to be constituted from, and to be embedded within, complex systems, risk is viewed as multifaceted rather than purely individualistic (Denny, 2005). In addition, risk is seen as contextualized, and it is to be expected that an adequate risk management plan would need to take into account individuals' particular lifestyles and environments. Even those dynamic risk factors that can be said to be located "inside" individuals (e.g. impulsivity, aggressiveness) are only meaningful in their specific, cultural and situational contexts. As such, etiological theories need to be explicitly ecological and multisystemic when seeking to formulate explanations of offending and its consequences, and the cultural dimensions of risk need to be considered when planning therapeutic interventions (see Lynch, 2006).

Finally, according to the GLM, a treatment plan should be *explicitly* constructed in the form of a good lives conceptualization. In other words, it should take into account individuals' strengths, primary goods and relevant environments, and specify exactly what competencies and resources are required to achieve these goods. An important aspect of this process is respecting the individual's capacity to make certain decisions himself or herself, and in this sense accepting his or her status as an autonomous individual. This is in direct contrast to previous recommended practice in the treatment of offending behaviors, where therapists were cautioned not to allow offenders to participate in decision-making (e.g. Salter, 1988). Using the GLM, we believe that each individual's preference for certain primary goods should be noted and translated into his or her daily routine (e.g. the kind of works, education and further training, and types of relationship identified and selected to achieve primary goods). This assumption is both normative and pragmatic. Normatively, we argue that individuals should not be forced to undergo changes in their character or core sense of self against their wishes. Pragmatically, we doubt whether such a thing is really possible, outside works of fiction like *A Clockwork Orange* (Burgess, 1962). In other words, self-change necessarily involves the motivation to change and requires that the client "buy in" to the change process (see Maruna, LeBel *et al.*, 2004). Even if there is no moral obligation for correctional practitioners to respect client autonomy and choice (and we argue that there is), rehabilitative success still likely requires it.

This final assumption has substantial implications for the nature and character of rehabilitative interventions. The GLM should be understood in the tradition of "rights-based" rehabilitation. That is, whereas some rehabilitation interventions are normatively justified on the grounds that the needs of the community outweigh the rights and liberties of the individual offender, others have justified rehabilitation itself as being the "right" of the prisoner or probationer (see e.g., Rotman, 1990; Lewis, 2005). That is, although no one should be obligated to undergo rehabilitation, the *state* is itself obligated to provide such help to those who want to change their life (see also Carlen, 1994; Cullen and Gilbert, 1982). The GLM falls squarely in this tradition. Individuals take part in GLM – as they might in education or other forms of self-improvement – because they think that such activities might either improve the quality of their life (intrinsic goal) or at least look good to judges, parole boards and family members (extrinsic goal).

ETIOLOGICAL ASSUMPTIONS OF THE GLM

As stated in Chapter 2, the etiological component of a rehabilitation theory flows logically from a theory's basic assumptions, is general in nature, and functions to give correctional workers a cognitive map or general overview of the broad causes of antisocial behavior. The etiological framework outlined here integrates aspects of various pre-existing theories of criminality in a way that is user-friendly for practitioners and (crucially) clients in a therapeutic situation. After all, etiological explanations need to be empirically valid, but also practically useful. They need to "make sense" to rehabilitation participants and lead naturally to practical intervention strategies. Like all behaviors, criminal behavior is a product of complex interactions between *biological* factors (influenced by genetic inheritance and brain development), *ecological* niche factors (i.e. social, cultural and personal circumstances) and *neuropsychological* factors. The role of an etiological theory is to organize these complex factors into a parsimonious and elegant "story" that is readily understandable by others.

Building on a central premise of "strain theory" (see Messner and Rosenfeld, 2001), the GLM proposes that crime might best be understood as the product of obstacles to the pursuit of legitimate goals. According to the GLM, goals are usefully construed as primary human goods translated into more concrete forms, and as such are typically the objects of intentions and actions. Goals are the ultimate and intermediate ends of any actions and collectively give shape to people's lives in so far as they create a structure of daily activities that represent what is of fundamental importance to them. Goals ultimately reflect the values individuals hold and are buttressed by beliefs about the social world and the people themselves. Problems in the scope of these goals, and the planning necessary to achieve them, can involve social, biological and psychological impediments.

Criminal behavior can be understood as the product of distortions in an individual's value/belief system. Yet the origins of these distorted self-narratives are always in the person's cultural environment. Self-identity is not constructed in a social vacuum (see Presser, 2004). Each of us draws on available cultural narratives in constructing our own worldviews. Thus, changing behaviors necessarily requires paying attention to both psychosocial functioning and ecological/cultural influences simultaneously.

According to the GLM, there may be a number of distinct problems within the various domains of human functioning that can result in offending behavior: emotional regulation difficulties, social difficulties, offense-supportive beliefs, empathy problems and problem-solving deficits. Yet such individuals' underlying personal motivations/goals are rarely inherently bad. Instead, it is the means used to achieve these goods that are deviant. The value of this understanding is that it helps to focus clinical attention on primary goods, the ultimate underlying motivating factors, and away from an exclusive focus on the (very real and important) psychosocial difficulties with which individual clients are struggling. That is, there are likely to be distortions in the internal and external conditions required to achieve the primary goods in socially acceptable and personally satisfying ways. Yet the GLM-guided analysis goes beyond deficit etiological theories (i.e. theories that focus on what individuals lack) by encouraging clinicians to think clearly about just what it is that the person is *seeking* when committing the offense. This information has direct treatment implications and can provide a powerful way of motivating individuals to engage in therapy; the aim is to help them to secure human goods that are important to them, but to do so in ways that are socially acceptable and also more personally satisfying. The latter point is especially important, as most of the causal factors involve self-defeating attempts to seek personally valued goals and consequences. The GLM can explain why this is so and provide clinicians with a clear understanding of where the problems reside in an individual's life plan.

From the perspective of the GLM, there are two routes to the onset of offending: direct and indirect (Purvis, 2005; Ward and Gannon, 2006). The *direct* pathway is implicated when offending is a primary focus of the (typically implicit) cluster of goals and strategies associated with an individual's life plan. This means the individual seeks certain types of good directly through criminal activity. For example, an individual may have compromised internal skills for gaining primary goods in more pro-social ways because of varied distal ecological factors. Thus, the actions constituting offending are a means to the achievement of a fundamental good. It must be stressed that the person concerned may be unaware of the primary good that is being sought, and simply be concerned with engaging in criminal behavior. In other words, sometimes the goals that actually motivate human actions (e.g. efforts to establish a sense of autonomy or power) are invisible to the individual in question.

The *indirect* route occurs when the pursuit of a good or a set of goods creates a ripple effect in the person's personal circumstances and these unanticipated effects increase the pressure to offend. For example, conflict between the goods of relatedness and autonomy might cause the break-up of a valued relationship and subsequent feelings of loneliness and distress. The use of alcohol to alleviate the emotional turmoil could lead to loss of control in specific circumstances, and this might increase the risk of offending. In this type of situation there is a chain of events initiated by the goods conflict that ultimately results in a risk of offending.

In the GLM, criminogenic needs are *internal* or *external obstacles* that frustrate and block the acquisition of primary human goods. What this means is that the individual concerned lacks the ability to obtain important outcomes (i.e. goods) in his or her life, and in addition is frequently unable to think about his or her life in a reflective manner. We suggest that there are four major types of difficulty often evident in individuals' life plans. In our view these types of problem are often overlapping but conceptually distinct. It is also important to note that the real problem resides in the secondary goods rather in than the primary ones. In other words, it is the activities or strategies used to obtain certain primary goods that create problems not the primary goods themselves (i.e. primary goods are sought by all humans). So an individual who has problems with the *means* he uses to secure goods may be using inappropriate strategies to achieve the necessary primary goods needed for a good life. An individual's life plan might also suffer from a lack of *scope*, with a number of important goods left out of his or her plan for living. For example, the good of work-related competence might be missing, leaving the person with chronic feelings of inadequacy and frustration. Some people may also have *conflict* (and a lack of coherence) among the goods being sought and therefore experience acute psychological stress and unhappiness (Emmons, 1999). An example of conflict in a life plan is where the attempt to pursue the goal of autonomy through attempting to control or dominate a partner makes it less likely goods related to intimacy will be achieved. A final problem is when a person lacks the *capabilities* (e.g. knowledge, skills) to form or implement a life plan in the environment in which he lives, or to adjust his or her goals to changing circumstances (e.g. impulsive decision-making). For example, a submissive individual may lack the skills to assert himself or herself sufficiently to get basic respect needs met from others. This lack of capability may lead to increased subjective emotional experiences of frustration and humiliation, which may be relieved or comforted through aggressive release. The problem of capability deficits has both internal and external dimensions. The internal dimension refers to factors such as skill deficits while the external dimension points to a lack of environmental opportunities, resources and supports.

In summary, the etiological commitments of the GLM are *general* in form and stem from a naturalistic view of human beings as goal-seeking, culturally embedded animals who utilize a range of strategies to secure important goods from their environment. When the internal or external conditions necessary to achieve valued outcomes are incomplete, individuals tend to become frustrated and may engage in antisocial behavior. The etiological commitments serve to orient correctional workers and require supplementation from specific theories to supply more fine-grained explanations.

IMPLICATIONS OF THE GLM FOR PRACTICE

A critical therapeutic task involves managing the balance between the approach goal of promoting personal goods and the avoidance goal of reducing risk. Erring on the side of either goal can result in disastrous social and personal consequences for the therapist and the client. Simply seeking to increase the well-being of a prisoner or a probationer without regard for his or her level of risk may result in a happy but dangerous individual. Alternatively, attempting to manage an individual's risk without concern for goods promotion or well-being could lead to punitive practices and a defiant or disengaged client (see Maruna, LeBel *et al.*, 2004; Sherman, 1993).

A related consideration concerns the attitude of the therapist to the client and the importance from the perspective of the GLM of adapting a constructive, humanistic relationship (see Chui and Nellis, 2003; Toch, 1997). The fact that the offender is viewed as someone attempting to live a meaningful worthwhile life in the best way he can in the specific circumstances confronting him or her reminds correctional workers that their clients are not moral strangers. That is, individuals who commit offenses act from a common set of goals stemming from their underlying human nature. They warrant our respect for their capacity to change and the fact that their offending is directly or indirectly associated with the pursuit of the ingredients of a good life. The fact that they have committed harmful actions does not suggest that they are intrinsically bad or destructive individuals. It is only the rarest of individuals whose motives are purely psychopathic and sadistic. Even the most destructive actions (e.g. the military slaughter of innocent civilians) are almost always motivated by ultimately noble goals, albeit through misguided and distorted means. The focus on achieving primary goods speaks directly to clients' self-interest and incentives for engaging in treatment. Individuals may be persuaded to change their behavior for primarily self-regarding reasons rather than from any charitable feelings for the "good of society". This is especially true considering that, in many cases, individuals feel that "society" has been anything but charitable to them! From a therapeutic perspective, it is the fact that such individuals are motivated to change and *engage* in the treatment process that is critical. Thus, even if some rare individual was intrinsically "evil" (e.g. psychopathically sadistic and unconcerned with others), it does not mean that they cannot be treated according to the GLM. By focusing on the promotion of client self-interests (in personally satisfying but also socially acceptable ways), the GLM could conceivably work with those with no empathy at all (if such individuals exist).

The GLM recommends that there should be some degree of tailoring of therapy to match individual clients' particular life plans and their associated risk factors (i.e. problems with the internal and external conditions). In other words, the individual's particular strengths, interests, values (weightings of goods), social and personal circumstances, and home environments should be taken into account when constructing a rehabilitation plan. Although GLM interventions may still be implemented in a systematic and structured way (like current standard RNR programs), therapeutic tasks within standard program modules should be shaped to suit the person in question based on their own life plan. For example, while an individual might receive a standardized social skills module, individualized self-directed tasks might be geared to his or her particular needs and issues.

Another area where attention needs to be paid is the language of treatment. Modern intervention texts repeatedly use language such as "deficit", "deviance", "distortion", and "risk" (e.g. see Salter, 1988). All such words are associated with negative evaluations or expectancies. The GLM is a positive model, based on the assumption that people are more likely to embrace positive change and personal development, and so the kinds of language associated with GLM interventions should be future-oriented, optimistic and approach-goal focused. Seligman and Peterson (2003, p. 306) argue that "Positive clinical psychology cannot progress too far so long as it uses the language of disease and deficiency". Language associated with avoidance goals should be changed to language associated with approach goals. Thus, "relapse prevention" could be retermed "self-management" or "change for life"; problems and deficits should be rephrased as approach goals and skills development. Program names should be changed to reflect the future-orientation of treatment as well, so names like "STOP" (a popular acronym) or "Stop It Now" could be changed to "Moving On" or "New Beginnings". The use of positive language has a compelling effect on those we treat. For example, in HM Prison Service in the United Kingdom, changing the term "dynamic risk factor" to "treatment need" has greatly facilitated collaboration in assessment and treatment (see Mann *et al.*, 2004) as well as being a more accurate description of the results of therapeutic assessment.

Applying the GLM to offender treatment requires the delineation of several considerations that could underlie the construction of a treatment program. These are:

1. Prisoners and probationers as whole individuals are more than the sum of their criminal record. They have expertise and a variety of strengths that can benefit

society. Interventions should promote and facilitate these contributions whenever possible.

2. At the same time, many prisoners and probationers are likely to have experienced adversarial developmental experiences, and have lacked the opportunities and support necessary to achieve a coherent life plan.

3. Consequently, such individuals lack many of the essential skills and capabilities necessary to achieve a fulfilling life.

4. Criminal actions frequently represent attempts to achieve desired goods but where the skills or capabilities necessary to achieve them are not possessed (direct route). Alternatively, offending can arise from an attempt to relieve the sense of incompetence, conflict or dissatisfaction that arises from not achieving valued human goods (indirect route).

5. The absence of certain human goods seems to be more strongly associated with offending: self-efficacy/sense of agency, inner peace, personal dignity/social esteem, generative roles and relationships, and social relatedness.

6. The risk of offending may be reduced by assisting individuals to develop the skills and capabilities necessary to achieve the full range of human goods.

7. Intervention is therefore seen as an activity that should *add to* an individual's repertoire of personal functioning, rather than as an activity that simply *removes* a problem or is devoted to *managing* problems, as if a lifetime of grossly restricting one's activity is the only way to avoid offending (Mann *et al.*, 2004).

In other words, a more "holistic" treatment perspective is taken, based on the core idea that the best way to reduce risk is by helping individuals live more personally fulfilling, successful and productive lives. In addition, therapy is tailored to each client's good lives plan while still being administered in a systematic and structured way. For normative and practical reasons, individual clients need only undertake those treatment activities that provide the ingredients of their own particular plan. At stake here is both the development of a therapeutic alliance and the fit between therapy and clients' specific issues, abilities, preferences and contexts. In the GLM, risk factors are regarded as internal and external obstacles that make it difficult for an individual to implement a good lives plan in a socially acceptable and personally fulfilling manner. Thus, a major focus is on the establishment of skills and competencies needed to achieve a better kind of life, alongside the management of risk. This *twin focus* incorporates the strengths of the relapse-prevention and capabilities approaches to treatment. It is also much easier to motivate individuals if they are reassured that the goods they are aiming for are acceptable; the problem resides in the way they are sought. Of course, sometimes individuals mistake the means (secondary goods) for the end (primary goods), and it may be necessary to spend quite a bit of time exploring the goods that underlie their offending behavior and the specific problems in their life plan. In the GLM approach, the goal is always to create new skills and capacities within the *context* of individuals' life plans and to encourage fulfillment through the achievement of human goods.

THE INTERVENTION AND ASSESSMENT PROCESS

We propose that motivating correctional clients and creating a sound therapeutic alliance are pivotal components of effective treatment and should not be viewed as of lesser importance than the application of treatment strategies and techniques (Ackerman and Hilsenroth, 2003; McMurran, 2002). Too often, rehabilitation research ignores the role of therapist interaction effects in impacting client self-concept (see Maruna, LeBel *et al.*, 2004). Carroll (1998, p. 6) warns that the "mere delivery of skills training without grounding in a positive therapeutic relationship [may] lead to a dry, overly didactic approach that alienates or bores most [clients] and ultimately has the opposite effect of that intended". Working collaboratively with clients in developing treatment goals results in a stronger therapeutic alliance (Mann and Shingler, 2006) and therapist features such as displays of empathy and warmth, and encouragement and rewards for progress facilitate the change process (Marshall, Serran, Fernandez *et al.*, 2003).

The fact that offenders have committed harmful acts means that therapists are often torn between two conflicting responses: (*a*) a desire to help the client change and (*b*) moral condemnation. Moral condemnation, whilst an understandable and socially normal response, can intrude seriously into collaborative and empathic working relationships. One need only look at the history of militaristic boot camps, "scared straight" programs, and some "hot seat"-type interventions associated with the early therapeutic communities to see the disastrous consequences of bullying, name-calling and verbal assaults in the name of "therapy" (e.g. see Lutz, 2006; Petrosino, Turpin-Petrosino and Fincknaeuer, 2000; White, 1998). Effective therapists must find ways of overcoming any tendency to favor this understandable desire for personal condemnation and abuse. The GLM can help negotiate the tension between these two types of value because of its recognition that offenders have value as human agents, and also by making their offending intelligible in the light of the pursuit of human goods (also see Braithwaite, 1989). The respect that prisoners and probationers are owed as human beings, in conjunction with the understanding that the establishment of a therapeutic relationship requires trust and openness, means that therapists need to create a constructive and positive environment.

A particular strength of the GLM is that it has a strong developmental and historical orientation, and therefore stresses the continuity between the "old" offending self and the construction of a new self. The continuity occurs because, according to the GLM, individuals' basic commitments and values (i.e. overarching goods) remain the same, and it is simply the means by which they are sought that is different. It is our commitments and associated life plans that define who we are, and provide a compass by which we navigate our way through life. Thus, in the GLM there is respect for individuals' history and past selves, which is in keeping with cultural and social perspectives that place great value on the past and its meaning.

ASSESSMENT

The collaborative approach of the GLM involves a commitment from the therapist to working transparently and respectfully, and to emphasizing that the client's best interests are to be served by the assessment process. Potential issues of risk and need are presented to the client as areas for collaborative investigation. Results of assessment procedures such as psychometric testing are discussed, and the client is invited to collaborate in drawing conclusions from them. An excellent account of how assessment procedures can be interpreted collaboratively is given in Miller and Rollnick (2002). Perhaps most relevant of all to the GLM, the client's strengths and life achievements are considered to be as important as his or her offense-related needs in determining his or her prognosis and treatment plan. Where the collaborative risk assessment process has been introduced as a conscious strategy, the early indicators are that relationships between treatment staff and clients are greatly improved, with a subsequent positive effect on motivation and retention in treatment (Mann and Shingler, 2006).

We support the RNR argument that risk, needs and responsivity are three major issues to be explored through assessment. However, we also recommend a fourth area for exploration: *priorities*. In our view, risk–need principles should be nested or embedded within a good lives framework. By this we mean that it is essential to assess a client's own goals, life priorities, and his or her aims for the intervention. In particular, it is essential to understand how a client prioritizes and operationalizes the primary human goods described earlier in this chapter. If this fourth area is not explored, offender assessment concentrates only on vulnerabilities and fails to recognize the importance of understanding how an individual can become fulfilled (Maruna, Porter and Carvalho, 2004). We therefore recommend that assessment of risk and vulnerability are balanced with an assessment of the individual's strengths, goals and conception of the good life (Ward and Stewart, 2003).

At present, there is no psychometric measure that can reliably make such assessments. Yet, even as such instruments emerge, a reliance on questionnaires may limit the depth of data gathered and the rapport established with the individual client (see Toch and Wilkins, 1985). As such, a clinical interview – old-fashioned and derided though it is – is the recommended approach. We have tried, and found ineffective, the method of presenting a list of primary human goods to correctional clients and asking them to choose their priorities. In our experience, such a task has been approached as if it was a test rather than an opportunity for self-exploration. In consequence, we recommend instead that an open-ended interview is conducted, where the assessor's intentions and the rationale for the interview are made transparent.

There are two primary procedures for identifying the major human goods that form the basis of individuals' core commitments. The first is to note what kind of goals are evident in their offense-related actions and general life functioning. This form of assessment strategy is similar to the scientific detection of fundamental goals and is based on careful observation guided by research findings and theory (e.g. Emmons, 1999). This requires a judgment about the intentions underlying individuals' behavior and their overall purposes in particular contexts. While goals cannot simply be inferred from behavior in any straightforward sense, it is clear that what people do in conjunction with the norms regulating particular interactions provides evidence concerning their goals. The second assessment strategy is to ask a series of increasingly detailed questions about the things (i.e. activities, situations, experiences) individuals value in their life and what they put their energies into day to day. Asking about family members and people they know whom they admire or dislike is quite helpful. Additionally, we have also found that extending the range of inquiries to the realm of the fictional can be useful at times. This may be achieved by asking clients what individuals – either fictional (e.g. from television, movies, novels, historical, etc.) or real (e.g. historical or public figures) – they most admire and why. Additional questions include: Who would they most want to be like, and why? Who would they most like not to resemble, and why? And so on. The advantage of these questions about "possible selves" (Oyserman and Markus, 1990) is that they can tap into individual fantasies and self-narratives or possible life scripts (see McAdams, 1985, 2006; Presser, 2004).

In order to make a more comprehensive assessment of each individual's potential for achieving a good life, the assessing clinician should have an understanding of the following areas:

1. Is there restricted scope? That is, is the individual focusing on some goods to the detriment of other goods, so

that his or her life seems to lack adequate balance and range of priorities? For instance, the individual may overemphasize mastery and underemphasize relationships, or favor knowledge but not pursue any form of creativity.

2. Are some human goods pursued through inappropriate means? That is, has the individual chosen strategies for achieving goods which have turned out to be counterproductive? For example, she or he may have chosen to pursue the goal of intimacy by adopting extremely controlling behaviors toward partners.

3. Is there conflict among the goals articulated? For instance, does the individual prioritize goals that cannot co-exist easily, such as wanting emotional intimacy with a romantic partner but also wanting sexual freedom and variety of partners? Or does she or he predominantly engage in everyday behaviors that are inconsistent with his or her higher-order goals, such as an individual who desires autonomy but is required to display considerable loyalty to an employer? Emmons (1999) has clearly described the stress that results from a lifestyle that is inconsistent with one's most valued goods.

4. Does the person have the capacity or capabilities to enact their life plan and achieve their stated life goals? Is the plan realistic in light of their abilities, likely opportunities, deep preferences, and values?

An exploration of a client's life plan can assist the clinician to formulate a rehabilitation plan that provides the opportunity for greater life satisfaction and well-being. If individuals are able to see how the plan will directly benefit them in terms of goods that they value, then the GLM suggests that they will be far more likely to engage enthusiastically in treatment. Given the importance of motivation and engagement to successful treatment outcomes (see Ward,

Mann and Gannon, 2007), it seems reasonable to assume that the perception of treatment relevance will be associated with reduced risk of further offending.

CASE FORMULATION

The above questions, in conjunction with a systematic assessment of an individual's social and psychological attributes, should result in a good-lives-oriented case formulation and an associated treatment plan. The basic steps in this process are as follows.

The *first phase* concerns the detection of the clinical phenomena implicated in individuals' offending. In other words, what kind of problems do they present with and what criminogenic needs are evident? In the *second phase* the function of the offending is established through the identification of the primary goods that are directly or indirectly linked to the criminal actions. What were they trying to achieve with their offending? In addition, the identification of the *overarching good* or value around which the other goods are oriented should also be ascertained. The overarching good informs therapists about what is most important in a person's life and hints at his or her fundamental commitments. It is strongly constitutive of personal identity and is a useful way of illuminating how the person sees his or her world.

At this phase of the assessment process, clinicians will have a good sense of why the person committed an offense, his or her level of risk, the flaws in his or her life plan, and whether or not the link between the client's pursuit of primary goods is directly or indirectly connected to the offending behavior. We propose that individuals who follow a *direct* route to offending are likely to have entrenched offense-supportive beliefs, approach goals, and/or marked deficits in their psychosocial functioning. They are also likely to be assessed as high risk, a factor that reflects their many years of offending. By way of contrast, individuals who have followed an indirect route are more likely to be assessed as moderate or lower risk, and have more circumscribed psychological problems (Purvis, 2005; Ward and Gannon, 2006).

In the *third phase*, therapists should identify the individuals' particular strengths, positive experiences, and life expertise (i.e. the means available to the person to achieve their stated goals). The *fourth phase* specifies how the identified primary and secondary goods can be translated into ways of living and functioning: for example, specifying what kind of personal relationships would be beneficial to the person concerned. In the *fifth phase*, identification of the contexts or environments the person is likely to be living in once he or she completes the program is undertaken. In the *sixth phase*, the therapist constructs a good lives treatment plan for the client based on the above considerations and information. Thus, taking into account the kind of life that would be fulfilling and meaningful to the individual (i.e. primary goods, secondary goods, and their relationship to ways of living and possible environments), the clinician notes the capabilities or competencies he or she requires to have a reasonable chance of putting the plan into action. A treatment plan is then developed.

INTERVENTION CASE EXAMPLES

In order to make the assessment and treatment aspect of the GLM a bit more concrete we shall briefly describe what we consider to be core or common problems associated with GLM offense routes and the treatment needs that are likely to follow from this. Of course, from the perspective of the GLM, individuals vary in terms of the problems evident in their life and their routes into criminality. Therefore, our comments are only meant to be illustrative and not unduly prescriptive. What follows are modified case histories of real individuals and their treatment within a GLM framework.

INDIRECT GOOD LIVES ROUTE

Peter is a 28-year-old man with one prior conviction for domestic violence. He has been living with his girlfriend for three years. For the past couple of years, Peter has been finding his job frustrating because he feels that he is always following orders and would much prefer to run his own business (*conflict in the Good Lives plan*). Like many former prisoners, he is a strongly independent man who enjoys setting his own priorities in work and in his personal life (*human goods preferences*). He tends to become resentful and angry if consistently told what to do and how to behave. Because Peter is spending vast amounts of time investigating the possibility of running a business, he is never at home (*lack of scope in the Good Lives plan*). Furthermore, he finds it difficult to manage his emotions and often strikes out at others, verbally or physically, to release these feelings of anger and resentment (*inappropriate means*).

On one occasion, he returns home late from work and argues with his girlfriend because of his continued absences. She complains that he is too aloof and never listens to her concerns. Peter is hurt and feels that his girlfriend does not respect his interests or appreciate his needs. As his mood worsens, he has thoughts of striking out at her. From his previous experiences in prison treatment, he realizes that he is having risky thoughts, and decides that he does not want to reoffend (*avoidant goal: key indicator of the indirect route to offending*). Despite his goal to avoid offending, his thoughts are constantly filled with physical vengeance, which makes him feel out of control and panicky. He decides to try to ignore his thoughts and feelings in the hope that they will go away (*under-regulation: problem in the action/control system*). This strategy proves unsuccessful, and Peter eventually strikes out at his girlfriend, leaving her in need of hospitalization. Immediately following the episode, he is filled with remorse and self-disgust, and resolves that he will never reoffend.

GLM treatment focus. Peter's indirect route to reoffending appears to have been the product of an inability to deal with turmoil stemming from a frustrated life plan due to lack of emotional regulation skills. The major source for his feelings of anger and resentment resides in his strong need to feel in control and independent, and sensitivity to being "unfairly" treated by others. The overarching goods for Peter appear to be agency and competency. These value commitments point to the nature of his personal identity as a hard-working, capable, independent man who does not tolerate being dominated and controlled by others. Treatment from a GLM perspective would seek to promote a more harmonious life plan in which all of the primary human goods are experienced in a fulfilling way (e.g. autonomy, relatedness), thus reducing stress and promoting emotional regulation (i.e. inner peace).

Peter appears to lack a sense of control and agency when faced with life difficulties. This is particularly difficult for him to tolerate given the value he places on feeling in control and respected by others. Thus, key interventions will revolve around teaching him skills such as problem solving, negotiation, and conflict resolution. It may be the case that finding an occupation that meets his strong independence needs would be helpful (although, of course, high unemployment rates or a changing economy may make this difficult). Peter also needs to be involved in emotional management training to help him learn about emotional states and identify the ones which place him at risk of offending (this will ensure that the primary good of inner peace is within Peter's grasp). Learning how to attain and manage external support from others will also be a useful skill for Peter to learn (i.e. intimacy skills). Mastery and agency appear to be his over-arching goods and thus will be the fulcrum of a Good Lives intervention plan; these goods strongly point to Peter's sense of identity as a competent and independent individual.

DIRECT GOOD LIVES ROUTE

Jim is a 42-year-old with a long history of abusing young boys. Jim finds it difficult to achieve meaningful intimate relationships with adults (*lack of skills, confidence or social opportunities to gain primary human goods pro-socially*) and thus prefers identifying with and associating with children (use of *inappropriate means to achieve primary human goods*). He likes interacting with children because he feels that he can care for them and help solve their problems (*human goods preferences*). Jim often spends time thinking about children and fantasizing about them sexually (*approach goal: key indicator of the direct route to sexual offending*). Often, he gets to know a child's parents with whom he is superficially acquainted in order to gain access to a potential victim in a babysitting role (*effective regulation*). During the first few instances of babysitting, Jim gradually gains the victim's confidence by playing computer games and giving the victim small games and treats. As soon as he establishes a bond with his victim and the victim's parents, he starts to introduce pornography during his babysitting visits. Once the victim is desensitized in this way, Jim starts to play sexual games with them, and continues offending because he believes that the child enjoys the sexual activity (*problem in perception*). Nevertheless, he usually lessens his risk of apprehension by offering the victim money to keep "their little secret". He is apprehended only when one victim informs a teacher of Jim's babysitting activities.

GLM treatment focus. Jim is unlikely to view his lifestyle as being problematic, because he holds entrenched problems in his perceptions (i.e. offense-supportive beliefs). Thus, a major challenge of GLM therapy would be to increase Jim's knowledge concerning the illegitimacy of engaging in sexual activity with children. This, of course, is in keeping with traditional risk-management approaches. Yet the language used in the GLM would be positive, and not directed at "reducing" or "eliminating" antisocial content. Instead, the focus would be directed at increasing and promoting knowledge and awareness. Using a GLM approach, the therapist would recognize that it is not the primary human goods sought that are problematic, but rather the means used to secure them.

Relatedness appears to be Jim's overarching primary good and therefore strongly constitutive of his identity. That is, he sees himself as a loving, caring person whose major values revolve around mixing with and relating to children. The challenge for therapy is to use this overarching value as the focus for an intervention plan and to find a pro-social and personally satisfying way to achieve it. One possibility is to teach Jim how to transfer his nurturing, listening and caring skills to a helping context that does not involve children. This will enable him to utilize his strengths, learn how to meet important needs in an adaptive fashion, and retain a valued aspect of his identity. It is one of the virtues of the GLM that it does not seek to create a deep fracture between an individual's "old me and new me"; rather it seeks to find better ways for individuals to realize their longstanding commitments and valued goals.

Thus, the main aim of therapy for Jim would be to focus on developing the relevant capabilities and internal skills necessary to pursue the primary good of relatedness in a personally fulfilling and socially acceptable way. With individuals such as Jim, who have deviant desires (i.e. are directly motivated to offend), a focus on promoting personal goods (alongside risk management) is also more likely to increase personal investment in therapy – something typically neglected in the risk–needs approach.

CONCLUSIONS

The GLM functions as regulatory ideal and is therefore deeply pragmatic. It asks therapists to develop an intervention plan that seeks to capitalize on individuals' interests and preferences and to equip them with the capabilities they need to realize their plan in the environment into which they are likely to be realized. Constraints relating to individuals' abilities, the provision of resources, and the degree of support in their environments moderate the nature of such plans. The aim is to promote what goals are possible, taking into account each individual's unique set of circumstances. The GLM builds upon the clinically useful RNR model, but transcends this model by focusing not just on risks but also on individual motivation to change. This subtle difference has substantial implications for the shape of treatment practice. Rehabilitation as a practice has become so focused on lowering risk and increasing community safety that it is easy to overlook a rather basic truth: prisoners and probationers want a better life, not simply the promise of a less harmful one. That is, correctional clients need a motivation for engaging in treatment beyond the avoidant goal of deterrence and the charitable goal of improving community safety. The GLM provides an incentive to change by focusing on the individual's own life goals as motivating factors for treatment. In the next chapter we shall critically evaluate the GLM and ascertain how it measures up to the RNR model of rehabilitation.

6

EVALUATING THE GOOD LIVES MODEL[1]

The GLM is a very new theory of offender rehabilitation and therefore is still at the point of being theoretically elaborated, debated and critiqued. It has been presented as a complementary theory to RNR because of its ability to include both goods-promotion and risk-management aims within its policy and practice guidelines. This enables correctional workers to employ empirically supported interventions to reduce risk in a way that capitalizes on clients' desires to live a worthwhile life.

Yet many questions remain about the model. First, can the model work? That is, will programs consistent with the GLM reduce the likelihood of individuals committing additional crimes and therefore ensure that the risk to the community is reduced? Second, how theoretically and empirically robust is the model? The key questions here revolve around the GLM's capacity to provide a comprehensive account of the rehabilitation process that is empirically supported and conceptually coherent. In what follows, we do our best to evaluate how the GLM performs with respect to each of the components of a rehabilitation theory laid out in Chapter 2 (basic assumptions, etiological commitments, and practice implications). Obviously, as advocates of the theory ourselves, we are not unbiased in our assessment here. As such, even though we shall aspire to highlight both lingering weaknesses as well as those aspects we view as the theory's key strengths, the main purpose of this chapter is to provide the empirical underpinnings for the model laid out in the previous chapter. This evidence-base is not anywhere near as impressive or compelling as that of RNR; however, we feel that this emerging research supports our argument in favor of enhancing or transcending the risk paradigm in rehabilitation theory.

BASIC ASSUMPTIONS AND VALUES

The GLM draws much of its theoretical distinction from its primary assumptions about human nature and its basic values regarding treatment practice. The GLM is unabashedly old-fashioned (at least pre-postmodern) in both regards, adopting an explicitly humanist conception of human development and social interactions. We view human beings as fundamentally social creatures, driven to find meaning in their life through social interaction and individual achievement. These assumptions have profound influence on the principles of the GLM.

THEORETICAL SCOPE

The GLM emerges out of two traditions in psychology, both with long and respected pedigrees. Most obviously, the theory has emerged out of the RNR model of evidenced-based correctional practice. Additionally, the GLM is a product of basic psychological research in "positive psychology" and strengths-based practices (see Seligman and Csikszentmihalyi, 2000). Although relatively new, the science of positive psychology is among the most important and fastest-growing theoretical and empirical movements in the social sciences in the past decade (see Linley and Joseph, 2004).

EVIDENCE FOR THE PRIMARY GOODS

The research literature on human needs and evolutionary psychology indicates that individuals are naturally inclined to seek certain ends (Arnhart, 1998; Emmons, 1999; Kekes, 1989). From a psychological perspective, Deci and Ryan (2000) have developed the Self-Determination Theory of needs, which states that human beings are inherently active, self-directed organisms who are naturally predisposed to seek autonomy, relatedness and competence. *Autonomy* refers to individuals' propensity to self-regulate and organize their experiences and to function as unified, integrated beings. *Relatedness* refers to individuals' propensity to establish a sense of emotional connectedness to other human beings and to seek the subsequent goals of feeling loved and cared for. *Competence* refers to the propensity to establish a sense of mastery in one's environment, to seek challenges and increasingly to master them.

The basic goods constitutive of human well-being are derived from categorical or basic needs, and these needs are assumed to be expressions of human nature (Ward and Stewart, 2003). However, the way they are met and the different ways of living available in the world reflect the contingencies of social and cultural circumstances. The nature of the primary goods sought by individuals, and their weightings, are formed in specific cultural contexts and represent individuals' interpretations of interpersonal and social events. This knowledge is clearly influenced by culturally derived beliefs, values and norms (D'Andrade, 1995).

There is a wealth of research indicating that well-being is associated with a number of primary goods and that humans are by nature goal-striving beings. The evidence for the primary goods is quite extensive and extends over a number of different disciplines including anthropology, social science, social policy, psychology, evolutionary theory, practical ethics and philosophical anthropology (e.g. Arnhart, 1998; Aspinwall and Staudinger, 2003; Bauer, McAdams and Sakaeda, 2005; Cummins, 1996; Emmons, 1999; Linley and Joseph, 2004; Murphy, 2001; Nussbaum, 2000; Rescher, 1993). In terms of the specific primary goods there is accumulating evidence for all the ones outlined earlier: life or healthy physical functioning (e.g. Martin, 2005; Kyvsgaard, 1991); play (e.g. Wrzesniewski, Roszin and Bennett, 2003); work (e.g. Theodossiou, 1997); autonomy or agency (e.g. Dobransky, 1999; Emmons, 1999); inner peace or emotional equilibrium (e.g. Kelly, 2003; Maruna, 2001); relatedness and community (e.g. Brerscheid, 2003); spirituality or meaning (e.g. Emmons, 2003); pleasure (e.g. Martin, 2005); creativity (e.g. Cassandro and Simonton, 2003); and knowledge (e.g. Emmons, 1999; Lippke, 2003). Again, the list of primary goods outlined in the GLM is not meant to be exhaustive but is simply illustrative of the kinds of activity and experience that have been reliably associated with well-being. The above evidence provides some support for the GLM claim that human goals are related to the striving for the above goods and that lives that lack the primary goods are more likely to be characterized by unhappiness and various problems in social functioning.

Further support for the ubiquity of goal- or goods-seeking behavior comes from the self-regulation literature (Austin and Vancouver, 1996). As Emmons (1996, p. 331) states, "why are goals important for well-being? Simply, it is because that is how people are designed. Goal-directedness is a human enterprise." Self-regulation consists of the internal and external processes that allow an individual to engage in goal-directed actions over time, and in different contexts

(Baumeister and Heatherton, 1996). This includes the initial selection of goals, as well as the planning, monitoring, evaluation and modification of behavior to accomplish one's goals in an optimal or satisfactory manner. Goals are key constructs in theories of self-regulation and function to guide the planning, implementation and evaluation of behavior. In essence, goals are desired states or situations (i.e. valued states or goods) that individuals strive to achieve or to avoid, and as such are important components of personality (Austin and Vancouver, 1996; Emmons, 1996). Arguably, they have their origin in basic human needs for autonomy, competence and relatedness (Deci and Ryan, 2000). When a goal is salient or is activated, it functions as a reference value or standard of comparison, and subsequent information concerning an individual's behavior (and its consequences) are compared to this standard.

NATURALISM

A real strength of the GLM rehabilitation theory is its naturalistic orientation. One of the core assumptions is that human beings have evolved to possess cognitive and decision-making capacities that enable them to meet their needs and to solve pressing environment problems (Sterelny, 2003). Beliefs function as cognitive maps that represent relevant aspects of the world, and values provide goals that guide individuals to pursue and secure a range of primary human goods. Beliefs, values and actions interact in a dynamic way to help organisms navigate their way in the world and to resolve problems posed by the environment (e.g. mate selection, conflict resolution, goods promotion, and the creation of social alliances). Thus, the GLM assumes that individuals are active, goal-seeking animals with the capacity to detect and pursue goods. It is an ecological, dynamic view of human behavior.

As indicated in Chapter 5, we do not assume an *evolutionary psychology* view of the mind (e.g. see Tooby and Cosmides, 1992). From the perspective of evolutionary psychology, psychopathology results from malfunctioning mental modules (e.g. failure of the theory of mind module in autism or sexual preference mechanisms in child molesters) or their activation in inappropriate environments or contexts (e.g. fear responses in benign situations). We believe that this kind of approach is too focused on what happens inside individuals and does not allow for the plasticity of human behavior and the influence of social and cultural learning and self-development.

Rather, we advocate a form of gene-culture co-evolution theory developed by Odling-Smee and colleagues (2003), called *niche construction* (Siegert and Ward, in press). According to Odling-Smee and colleagues, niche construction occurs when organisms alter the environment and thereby modify the relationship between their characteristics and the features of the environment. Examples of niche construction in human beings are the building of houses, implementation of farming practices (e.g. dairy farming) and the development of technology. All these changes modify the niche in which human beings live and thereby change the relationship or match between humans and features of the environment. According to Odling-Smee and his associates, there are three types of process involved in niche construction in a population of diverse phenotypes (living organisms): *genetic processes, ontogenetic processes* (individual learning within a lifetime) and *cultural processes*. Each of these processes is associated with unique ways of acquiring, storing and transmitting information, and also with distinct means of interacting with the environment.

It is possible to utilize niche construction theory to understand psychological and social problems such as the predisposition of some individuals to engage in criminal activity. Take, for example, the issue of sexual assault. An example of a genetic predisposition might be males' hypothesized tendency to seek impersonal sex and also to attempt to exert power and control over females (Ward, Polaschek and Beech, 2006). An example of an ontogenetic process leading to impersonal sex could be learning to use sex as a way of coping with negative mood states and feelings of inadequacy. An example of a relevant cultural process might be the portrayal of females as sexual objects and males as sexually entitled to have sex when and where they want. A strength of the niche construction perspective is that it views humans naturalistically and hence resonates with a broad range of sciences while also respecting the critical role of social and cultural processes in generating behavior. Furthermore, values are tied to natural facts in a way that is scientifically and philosophically defensible (see below). These aspects of the GLM indicate its external consistency, explanatory depth, heuristic power and empirical adequacy. Human beings are conceptualized as "unfinished animals" who are scaffolded by social factors and also in turn partially shape the direction of their life.

VALUES AND PRACTICE

Another strength of the GLM is the attention it gives to values and their relationships to correctional practice. As stated earlier, value judgments reveal what individuals consider to be of worth (and beneficial) or of little value (and therefore harmful). In essence, value judgments reflect what overarching ends are considered good and worth seeking, all things being equal. In our view, values are partially "object-ive" in the sense that individuals can be mistaken about what experiences and situations *actually do* benefit or harm them. Moreover, we assert that human nature is such that people require certain experiences, activities or states of affairs (i.e. primary goods) in order for their lives to go well. These are likely to include relationships, leisure, a sense of belonging to a community or group, physical health, knowledge, agency and work.

According to the GLM, the impact of different types of value on correctional practice is evident in a variety of ways. *Cognitive* values (i.e. what constitutes good knowledge and how to secure it) help researchers and clinicians identify effective interventions and ways of helping individuals to desist from further offending. *Prudential* values (i.e. what kinds of experience, etc., are likely to result in enhanced well-being) partially determine the ultimate ends of correctional programs and facilitate the tailoring of specific interventions to match individuals' interests and emerging concerns. They also play a crucial role in motivating individuals to engage in treatment and form the core of a more adaptive narrative identity. *Ethical* values (i.e. regulation of the behavior of individuals toward others; what is right or wrong, good or bad) constrain the way practitioners behave toward clients and also provide limiting conditions for any program.

The GLM view of values is a naturalistic one that emphasizes the strong connection between facts associated with well-being and therapeutic actions. Values are therefore seen as objective and related to the various social, biological, cultural and psychological variables that culminate in, and eradicate, criminal actions. The aim of therapy should be to use information concerning the internal and external conditions reliably associated with human benefits and harms in order to provide individuals with better-quality and less destructive lives. Questions about the causes of crime and how to prevent it are always underpinned by values: we seek to explain offending because we are distressed by the misery that is created by antisocial behavior.

RELATIONSHIP BETWEEN RISK AND GOODS

According to the GLM, there is a causal relationship between human goods and risk factors. Human needs are met through the securing of primary human goods, that is, intrinsically valuable experiences or activities that are sought for their own sake. However, motivation on its own is not sufficient to realize valued outcomes; simply desiring a good does not guarantee that it can be achieved. What is required to attain primary goods is a combination of internal conditions (abilities, beliefs, etc.) and external conditions (opportunities, support, etc.). For example, in order to experience the various goods associated with intimate relationships individuals have to possess certain social skills, believe they are worthy of care and, crucially, have access to others who are actually interested in becoming involved with them. Criminogenic needs are conceptualized as internal or external obstacles that make it difficult for individuals to meet their needs. In other words, the distorted, incomplete or problematic internal and external conditions are the same thing as criminogenic needs. Thus, the criminogenic need of antisocial peers indicates that offenders may lack access to pro-social peers or else lack the necessary skills or confidence to establish such relationships. Likewise, the criminogenic need of impulsivity points to problems in achieving the good of autonomy. That is, the person concerned experiences difficulty in formulating and carrying out a plan successfully perhaps because he finds it hard to inhibit strong emotions or else has little experience of effective decision-making.

Therefore, an additional strength of the GLM is that it is able to explain how primary human goods and dynamic risk factors are connected. It also provides an account of how the various types of criminogenic need are linked and result in antisocial behavior; they represent maladaptive instrumental goods. Thus, careful scrutiny of a criminogenic need is likely to reveal that it is an inappropriate way of securing goods, either because the individual lacks the requisite capabilities or else his environment actively frustrates and defeats his best efforts. This feature of the GLM heralds its internal consistency and explanatory depth.

NARRATIVE IDENTITY IN THE CHANGE PROCESS

A unique feature of the GLM is the way narrative or personal identity concerns are built into the foundations of the theory. This is because of its emphasis on prudential values (primary goods) and the link between their weightings and individuals' sense of themselves. A notable feature of the stress on value commitments and actions is that human beings are viewed as dynamic and agentic entities who actively construct lifestyle plans and life worlds (Brandstadter, 1999; McAdams, 2006). At the same time, in order to construct viable identities people draw on the discursive (sources of meaning) resources in their social and cultural environment. Impoverished resources equate to unsatisfactory self-conceptions and frustrated, limited lives. An advantage of relating values and identity in this manner is that it establishes a conduit between the micro level of risk factors and the macro level of lifestyle and meaning. The connecting thread is via the notion of primary goods, personal goals and their embedding within an implicit or explicit life plan.

RISK AS MULTIFACETED

In previous chapters we criticized the conception of risk inherent in RNR, arguing that it was excessively narrow. In our view, risk is a multifaceted concept and therefore should contain individual, social, physical (situational) and cultural components. Risk is also a dynamic concept, and risk assessments should always be contextually and temporally tagged. One of the strengths of the GLM is that its metaphysical assumptions about the nature of human beings and their relationship to the environment directly entail a complex view of hazards and their assessment (i.e. risk assessment and management). From the point of view of the GLM, social and cultural factors may sometimes intervene to create or elevate risk estimates by virtue of their generation of hazards. For example, overly punitive parole conditions can function to stigmatize and isolate parolees from meaningful social relationships, therefore making it practically impossible for them to meet their needs for intimacy with others. Furthermore, environmental conditions can also create hazards that can eventually result in criminal actions. For example, the lack of adequate housing may result in crowded living situations and intense frustration, exacerbating already fraught relationships. One consequence of this type of frustration may be aggressive behavior. Finally, risk can also be located within individuals in the form of relatively stable personality traits or features, for example, antisocial attitudes, poor emotional control, or high levels of impulsivity. The fact that the GLM has a complex understanding of risk is therefore directly related to its conception of offenders (and for all people) as physically embodied and embedded in multiple systems, and exhibiting a high degree of interpersonal interdependence.

CONCLUSIONS

Assessing the strengths and weaknesses of GLM's theoretical assumptions is a difficult task, because these assumptions are just that – assumptions – even if based on inconclusive research evidence. The point of this evaluation is not to determine if various assumptions (e.g., that offenders are like everyone else and strive to live a good life) are "right" or "wrong", but rather whether or not they are consistent, reasonable and, most importantly, therapeutically useful. We argue that they are all of these things.

In a sense, the strengths of the GLM outlined above can also be viewed as potential weaknesses. After all, many of the above assumptions are strongly contested by theorists and researchers. Although they are underpinned by empirical findings, it is still possible to adopt a different view of phenomena such as risk, the role of values, and the relationship between goods and risks. Additionally, it could be argued that the definition of primary human goods in the GLM is problematic because it actually contains two, somewhat contrasting interpretations of this idea. On the one hand, primary goods are defined as activities, experiences, etc., that are sought for their own sake, linking their status as primary goods with a valuation of intrinsic motivation. On the other hand, primary goods are also viewed as experiences, etc., that are beneficial to human beings and that increase their welfare. The problem is that these two ways of defining primary goods are not necessarily coupled, and it is possible that a person may find some type of harmful or criminal activity to be intrinsically motivating. This issue points to a possible lack of internal coherence in the theory.

While we appreciate this point, our view is that there is frequently a connection between the two senses of primary goods: individuals seek certain activities and experiences for their own sake *because* they are beneficial. In other words, intimacy is regarded as a primary good and therefore a reason for action because the consequences of being in a loving relationship with another person are very rewarding. Thus, for human beings, (prudential) intrinsic value is strongly associated with the concept of personal well-being.

ETIOLOGICAL COMMITMENTS

There are essentially three etiological components in the GLM, claims that (*a*) individuals seek a number of primary goods in their offending, (*b*) there are different routes to offending, direct and indirect, and (*c*) criminogenic needs are best-understood as distortions in the internal and external conditions required to achieve primary human goods (or meet basic human needs). This final claim also encompasses the assertion that there are problems of scope, conflict, means and capacity associated with offenders' lifestyle plans. We shall now consider the theoretical merits and empirical evidence underlying these claims.

PRIMARY GOODS AND OFFENDING

The first line of evidence comes from the research cited above in support of the primary goods. We have made the assumption that offenders by virtue of being human have the same essential nature and needs as non-offenders. Furthermore, we have assumed that problems of conflict, scope, and lack of goods are likely to result in lower levels of well-being. For example, research evidence suggests that happy people (people with high levels of well-being) exhibit, on average, more adaptive behaviors, are more productive and more sociable (Diener, 2000).

More direct evidence, however, comes from criminological research on the process of desistance from crime. One of the best-known facts in criminology is that the majority of one-time criminal offenders eventually "grow out" of criminal behavior and "go straight". Criminal-career researchers have estimated that approximately 85 percent of crime-involved young people will desist by the time they are 28 years old (e.g. see Blumstein and Cohen, 1987). Rather than being a "natural" or biological process, however, desistance appears to be a normative transition, linked to other culturally sustained and biologically influenced developmental milestones (see Maruna, 2001). In general, efforts to "unpack" this age–crime relationship have been dominated by three basic paradigms: informal social control theory, differential association theory, and variations of symbolic interactionist or socio-cognitive theories (for a more complete review, see Farrall and Calverley, 2006; Laub and Sampson, 2001).

Although sometimes put into competition against one another, all of these plausible theoretical frameworks are largely compatible, with more essential commonalities than differences. In particular, all these accounts, in some way or another, reflect the fulfillment of human needs for "agency" and "communion" (Bakan, 1966) in the desistance process. That is, each theory predicts that desistance should be associated with the achievement of competence, autonomy and success in the pro-social world (usually in the form of a career) and the development of intimate interpersonal bonds (usually in the form of a family). That such things are important to one's ability to go straight is hardly surprising. Sigmund Freud nominated these two aspects of life – work and love – as the two essential ingredients of a happy and well-adjusted personality.

If it is true that human beings have a natural predisposition "to experience themselves as causal agents in their environment", and to earn the esteem and affection of valued others (Gecas and Schwalbe, 1983, p. 78), then crime might be associated with constraints on these human needs. For instance, Moffitt (1993, pp. 686–7) describes the 5-to-10-year role-vacuum that teenagers and young adults face during which "they want desperately to establish intimate bonds with the opposite sex, to accrue material belongings, to make their own decisions, and to be regarded as consequential by adults" only to find they are "asked to delay most of the positive aspects of adult life". When social structures constrain one's ability to achieve agency and autonomy (or, in Marxist terms, when the individual is alienated from his or her labors), an individual might turn to criminal or delinquent behaviors in order to "experience one's self as a cause" rather than an "effect" (Matza, 1964, p. 88; see also Messner and Rosenfeld, 2001). Conversely, and logically, desistance from crime may be facilitated when the individual finds an alternative, intrinsically rewarding source of agency and affiliation. Trasler (1980) writes: "[A]s they grow older, most young men gain access to other sources of achievement and social satisfaction – a job, a girlfriend, a wife, a home and eventually children – and in doing so become gradually less dependent upon peer-group support" (cited in Gottfredson and Hirschi, 1990, p. 135; see also Laub and Sampson, 2001). Additionally, the desisting individual may find some sort of "calling" – be it parenthood, painting, coaching, or what Richard Sennett (2003) calls "craft-love" – outside the criminal world through which they find meaning and purpose outside crime.

In fact, emerging criminological research can provide some (weak) support for the link between the attainment of each of the primary human goods and criminal behavior. The list below provides just a small sample of some of the possible studies in this regard:

- *Quality of life-health*: There are numerous links between quality of life and criminality. Kyvsgaard (1991) found that offenders experienced more material deprivation than the general population and that there was a significant correlation between the severity of crime and the degree of deprivation. Moreover, there appears to be a strong correlation between depression and persistent offending (see Chiles, Miller and Cox, 1980; Capaldi,

1992; Maruna, 2004; McLeod and Shanahan, 1993; McManus *et al.*, 1984).

- *Mastery*: Steady, gainful employment has long been linked to desistance from criminal behavior (see Kruttschnitt, Uggen and Shelton, 2000; Ouimet and Le Blanc, 1996; Sampson and Laub, 1993).
- *Agency*: Research has consistently found that impulsivity is a strong predictor of future offending (Andrews and Bonta, 2003), and desistance research has confirmed the importance of feelings of control over one's future in aiding the reintegration process (see Laub and Sampson, 2001; Maruna, 2001).
- *Inner peace*: The important role of emotional regulation (inner peace) in triggering offending has been revealed by research on sexual offending (Bumby and Hansen, 1997) and violent offenders (King, 2001).
- *Relatedness*: Marriage and stable relationships have a demonstrable impact on recidivism patterns (Andrews and Bonta, 2003; Laub, Nagin and Sampson, 1998; Marshall, 1999; Marshall, Anderson and Fernandez, 1999; Marshall and Marshall, 2000).
- *Spirituality*: In a study on sex offenders, Geary (2002) concluded that spirituality and church attendance were positively associated with higher levels of well-being.
- *Creativity*: Some research suggests that engaging in creative pursuits is also therapeutically useful as it imparts a sense of meaning (Liebmann, 1994; Maruna, 2001).

Although each of these areas of research requires further development, the above empirical evidence does provide some support for the GLM etiological claims concerning primary human goods and lifestyle problems. In addition, the vast amount of work on human needs, subjective well-being, quality of life, and personal strivings (among the wider, "non-offender" population) is clearly relevant and strongly suggests that individuals' levels of well-being and happiness are linked to personal goals and their achievement (e.g. Cummins, 1996; Emmons, 2003). The important remaining question, however, is *how* this well-being is linked to reoffending and community safety.

DIRECT AND INDIRECT ROUTES

We have argued that there are two routes between goods attainment and the onset of offending: direct and indirect. This argument is based on research by Ward and colleagues on the offense chain in sexual offending (e.g. Purvis, 2005; Ward and Gannon, 2006; Ward and Hudson, 2000). Ward and Hudson (2000) developed an alternative approach to the treatment of sexual offenders based on self-regulation theory (Baumeister and Heatherton, 1996; Thompson, 1994). The self-regulation model was explicitly developed to account for the variety of offense pathways evident in sexual offenders and to provide therapists with a more comprehensive treatment model (Ward *et al.*, 2004). Ward's Self-Regulation Model (SRM) posits nine phases in the offense progression and four distinct pathways that lead to sexual offending. For example, the *avoidant-passive* pathway is characterized by the desire to avoid sexual offending; however, the individual lacks the coping skills to prevent this from occurring (i.e. under-regulation). Alternatively, the *approach-explicit* pathway is characterized by the desire to sexually offend, the use of careful planning to execute offenses, and the presence of harmful goals concerning sexual offending. There have been four empirical evaluations of the validity of the SRM, all concluding that it is supported by the evidence (for a summary of these studies, see Ward *et al.*, 2004; Ward, Yates and Long, 2006). While these studies have not directly tested the finding that sexual offending is at least partly related to inappropriate pursuit of human goods, the relationship between approach goals and personal goals provides at least weak evidence for the GLM etiological claims concerning offending and goods (goals).

Moreover, this research suggests that some individuals directly seek certain types of goal in their offending, for example, a sense of belonging or emotional relief. For these individuals it was clear that their sexually abusive behavior was utilized as a way of meeting certain needs. However, for other individuals, the pathway from nonoffending to sexually abusive behavior was more indirect. Typically, it involved a kind of ripple effect where a person's inability to achieve valued outcomes due to lack of skills or the use of inappropriate means resulted in lifestyle problems and subsequent dissatisfactions. This initial dissatisfaction then led to downstream problems that ultimately culminated in a sexual offense. An important finding was that, while individuals tended to follow both direct and indirect routes (via each of the goods), typically they could be allocated into one of the pathways based on their overall picture (Purvis, 2005).

Importantly, the theoretical arguments linking the GLM and the SRM are only conceptual in nature. The empirical evidence for two routes rests on the data from the SRM studies and the preliminary work of Purvis (2005), both of which involve sex offenders and so cannot be easily generalized to the wider offender population. The theoretical advantages indicate the GLM's relative simplicity concerning offense routes and its internal consistency and coherence. However, the lack of research data directly evaluating the two-route claim means that at this stage its empirical support is rather weak and tentative.

CRIMINOGENIC NEEDS AND INTERNAL/ EXTERNAL CONDITIONS

From the perspective of the GLM, risk factors and goals are linked through individuals' inability to realize personal goals in more adaptive and socially acceptable ways. A major feature of the GLM is the way it unpacks the notion of criminogenic needs in terms of internal and external conditions. This is essentially a theoretical move and should be evaluated in terms of whether or not it manages to solve certain theoretical puzzles that are apparent in RNR. These revolve around RNR's failure to (*a*) explain adequately how human needs and other motivational constructs are related to criminogenic needs; (*b*) account for the relationship between various criminogenic needs; and (*c*) understand how criminogenic needs result in criminal activities. We shall briefly address each of these issues in turn and demonstrate how the GLM analysis of criminogenic needs might effectively deal with these problems.

According to the GLM, in order to achieve primary goods effectively in particular circumstances, it is necessary to meet two sets of conditions. First, individuals require the capabilities or skills required to perform goal-directed actions and, by doing so, engage in the valued activity or else reach it via a series of secondary steps. Second, in order to meet human needs it is necessary to have access to relevant opportunities, and to be supported – or, at the very least, not thwarted – by others in the process. Deficits in either of these two sets of factors would therefore make it unlikely that a person would be able to achieve what he set out to. He or she would be unable to have his or her needs met and therefore to secure the relevant primary goods. Criminogenic needs constitute the relevant deficits in the internal and external conditions.

Take, for example, the risk factor of impaired social

competency. From an *etiological* perspective, the overarching goods associated with social competency are those of relatedness, community connectedness, emotional regulation, and agency (autonomy). A lack of intimacy, emotional regulation and communication skills makes it difficult for individuals to achieve satisfactory relationships with adults, and therefore other avenues for meeting such needs are explored (internal condition deficits). Furthermore, a history of abuse or neglect can leave a legacy of distrust and fear, deterring individuals from attempting to get close to people from their own age group (external condition deficit).

In terms of how criminogenic needs are interrelated, the unifying construct is that of lifestyle and the particular contexts within which individuals live. According to the GLM, primary human goods are actively sought and motivate individuals to undertake activities of various kinds: establishing relationships, tackling achievement tasks, indulging in leisure activities, and so forth. The natural inclination to seek primary goods means that people are constantly looking for ways to achieve their goals and to implement their various projects. Projects embody interests and concerns that structure people's day-to-day actions and in this sense shape their lives. These attempts might be explicit and therefore objects of awareness or else remain implicit and only recognizable as goal-directed behavior on reflection. Whether or not such "projects" are consciously formulated and planned or else given to individuals by their social environment, one thing is clear: the way a person lives is a function of his or her values (goods, goals, etc.), capabilities, opportunities and social/cultural contexts. To put it metaphorically, lifestyles are braided rivers within which the various tributaries (diverse goods and their associated actions) converge to produce direction and momentum.

Criminogenic needs generate antisocial actions through their expression within individual lifestyles. On some occasions the natural inclination to seek relatedness can result in a decision to socialize with antisocial peers. The person concerned might lack the opportunities and/or the capabilities (skills, attitudes, beliefs) to integrate with other groups. Thus, offenses are partially determined by problematic internal and/or external conditions.

PRACTICE IMPLICATIONS

The GLM is a wide-ranging theory of rehabilitation and as such has specific intervention implications that stem from both its core set of assumptions and values, and its etiological commitments. It manages to integrate aspects of practice that are viewed as important by correctional workers but which RNR does not deal with particularly well. These include: the importance of identity formation; motivating individuals to participate in correctional work; accounting for the importance of the therapeutic alliance (noncriminogenic needs); working in a more holistic, constructive way; providing tailored, flexible intervention approaches; and clarifying the role of values in the change process. We shall now briefly evaluate the significance of these features.

IDENTITY FORMATION

Because the GLM is an ecological model, it stipulates that an adequate understanding of individuals and their antisocial behavior requires engaging in both horizontal and vertical levels of analysis. The horizontal level of analysis involves the various systems an individual actor is embedded in. A useful metaphor is that of widening concentric circles, like ripples in a pond (see Bronfenbrenner, 1979). The vertical level of analysis refers to the various psychological and physical systems and processes that collectively constitute a person and interact to produce behavior. A helpful metaphor here is that of a fishing net, with each strand connected to all the others. Because the GLM views human beings as essentially embodied agents existing within a network of social, cultural and physical relationships, it is assumed that there is rarely a single cause of any aberrant action. Narrative identity emerges from the individual's understanding of where he or she is located within this array of relationships and what particular goals (goods) are most important to him or her. The construct of *offender lifestyles* provides a way of linking the various levels and variables together; there is an appreciation of the environment (physical and cultural), goals, and internal and external conditions that make goal achievement possible. Narrative identity is intimately connected to an individual's lifestyle and its various component parts, individual features, opportunities, cultural and physical processes.

Therefore, it is argued that focusing on single risk factors may result in a fractured, piecemeal approach to intervention. By taking seriously the relationship between narrative identity, primary goods (values) and lifestyle, therapists are able to assess clients as "whole" people and to build an intervention plan around them. To illustrate how this process works, consider the following GLM case intervention provided by Whitehead and his colleagues (Whitehead, Ward and Collie, in press). The client was a longtime gang member with a long history of violence who had attended several criminogenic programs without much success. During his goals assessment, the client told his counselor that a longstanding ambition was to attend university, but he did not feel this would ever be possible. An intervention program was formulated with this long-term goal as its basis. In order to be able to enroll for a pre-university course he needed to work on his social skills and anger management, change his attitude toward others and improve his time-keeping. Gradually, the internal and external conditions required to reach the goal of university attendance successfully were put in place and the individual's sense of who he fundamentally was began to change. He left the gang and started to view himself as a knowledge-seeker, someone who was capable of learning and could apply his knowledge in constructive ways.

At the moment, all such GLM assessments are made using clinical interviews, and therefore require quite a degree of clinical sophistication. There are no self-report scales to help in this process, although a number of semi-structured and coding systems are in use and are currently being developed. In the mean time, one useful strategy is to use criminogenic needs as range riders. By this we mean as indicators that there are problems in the way goods are being sought. For example, the criminogenic need of social incompetence indicates problems in meeting relatedness needs, while that of impulsivity strongly suggests problems with emotional regulation (inner peace and autonomy). Thus, it is possible to use existing, dynamic measures of risk (e.g. the Level of Service Inventory-Revised) to detect criminogenic needs, as long as the clinician then probes more deeply into the nature of the need, asking: "What goods is this compromising and is it a problem of means, capacity, scope, or conflict?"

APPROACH AND AVOIDANCE GOALS

The GLM starts with basic assumptions stressing the importance of enhancing the quality of clients' lives and helping them to achieve personal goals alongside the management of risk. The attention to both goods promotion and risk reduction enables the GLM to deal with issues of motivation, identity and lifestyle. RNR struggles with these clinical concerns because its primary orientation is toward risk reduction and it tends to downplay the welfare of offenders in favor of the good of the community. Our argument is that it is possible (indeed, crucial) to have a twin focus on motivation as well as on risk (that is, approach as well as avoidance goals) in rehabilitation practice and that neglecting either is potentially dangerous. We argue that, when primary goods are promoted in a systematic way, risk is automatically reduced.

The aim is to instill in prisoners and probationers the competencies they require to establish the depth, range and kinds of relationship likely to enhance their well-being and that are congruent with their overall good lives plan. A somewhat neglected aspect of social competence work concerns the external conditions necessary for a person to function effectively within his social, cultural and physical environment. This would involve ensuring that the individual has the opportunities to develop friendships and connectedness to the community and move away from deviant peer associations. Thus, equipping treatment clients with the internal and external conditions needed to secure social goods is also likely to reduce or modify those criminogenic needs revolving around interpersonal issues.

The relationship between approach/avoidance goals and criminal outcomes is an empirical issue, and at this stage the evidence is only indirect. Certainly the evidence from research on approach and avoidance goals in a variety of domains outside criminology supports our general argument (e.g. Austin and Vancouver, 1996; Emmons, 1999; Gable, 2006). For example, Gable (2006) found that facilitating the achievement of approach social goals reduced loneliness more effectively than simply seeking to avoid loneliness and relationship insecurity. In view of our contention that loneliness (or social isolation) is a criminogenic condition, this is a relevant finding and is consistent with the GLM argument.

More directly relevant, Mann and colleagues (2004) have developed a way of teaching relapse prevention based on approach goals, rather than using the risk reduction approach seen in the majority of programs. Treatment clients are taught to distinguish between approach and avoidance goals and to set subgoals that would enable them to establish a "new me" (i.e. a more adaptive personal identity). The kind of approach goals formulated included the development of better adult relationships, rather than simply avoiding reoffending and risky behaviors. This approach was found to be clinically effective and also created a more positive therapeutic environment (Mann *et al.*, 2004).

THERAPEUTIC ALLIANCE

The GLM places great stress on the importance of establishing a therapeutic alliance with treatment clients, and in this respect considers noncriminogenic needs such as personal distress and self-esteem to be of direct relevance. The point here is that in order to motivate individuals to initiate and maintain change it is first necessary to create a good relationship and for the person to feel that change agents trust and respect them. Research suggests that efforts to increase offenders' self-esteem facilitate the primary targets of therapy and that working collaboratively with offenders in developing treatment goals results in a stronger therapeutic alliance (Mann *et al.*, 2004). Furthermore, empathetic, warm therapists who encourage and reward progress appear to be the most effective in motivating change (Marshall, Fernandez, Serran *et al.*, 2003).

The GLM helps practitioners focus on the "humanity" of offenders, thereby making their offenses more transparent and understandable. This is likely to help them to distinguish carefully between individuals' character and their behavior, and also to balance therapeutic and moral values.

RNR struggles with this issue because of the primary emphasis on risk reduction and potential harm to the community. The difficulty is that viewing offenders exclusively through a risk lens means that it is more difficult to see their value as human beings and easier to regard them in rather punitive terms (see especially Hannah-Moffat, 2005). Of course it is possible to argue that there is nothing in RNR to exclude attending to noncriminogenic needs. Indeed, the responsivity principle is primarily concerned with the process of program engagement and delivery. Therefore, it might be asserted that the GLM offers nothing additional here. The issue is that RNR sees such attention as discretionary whereas the GLM makes attending to the therapeutic relationship a mandatory aspect of effective interventions.

INTEGRATED HOLISTIC APPROACH

A notable feature of the GLM is the way it integrates internal and external conditions and also adopts a dynamic ecological view of etiology and intervention. It reminds practitioners that it is important to consider a wide range of individual interests and to pay particular attention to the values (goods) they weight most highly. The search for primary human goods and their role in individuals' lives helps to adopt a comprehensive and integrated view of both etiology and intervention and to avoid a simplistic reductionistic perspective on reintegration. One risk of such a holistic approach, however, is that practitioners can lose focus and cast their therapeutic net too widely. Also, careful analyses of the different domains of offenders' lives could prove to be rather expensive in terms of resources and time.

TAILORING

In our view, one of the great virtues of the GLM is the way it can amalgamate manual-based and more individually tailored approaches to intervention. Once certain types of programs have been identified as effective in reducing or modifying specific risk factors, a good lives or lifestyle formulation is developed that constellates standard intervention techniques around a set of primary and instrumental goods. For example, a person with a history of violent crimes might receive standard anger management techniques but geared toward his overall goal of, for instance, finding employment or starting a family. The merit of this type of integration is that it addresses responsivity issues and helps to focus interventions around genuine concerns of correctional clients.

EFFECTIVENESS OF GLM INTERVENTIONS

For some, none of the preceding issues is anywhere near as important as the crucial question: "Does the bloody thing work?" To date, it is too early to answer this conclusively. The GLM is starting to be utilized in interventions addressing violence, sex offending and general offending behavior in a number of countries throughout the world. These include Ireland (sex offenders), England (adult and adolescent sex offenders, general forensic patients), Canada (adult sexual offenders), Australia (adult and adolescent sex offenders, general offenders), New Zealand (adult sexual and nonsexual offenders, intellectually disabled offenders, adolescent offenders) and the United States (sexual and nonsexual offenders, forensic mental health patients). Evaluations are only just beginning, but very preliminary results have been promising. Lindsay, Ward, Morgan and Wilson (2006), for instance, found that utilizing the principles of the GLM in conjunction with accepted relapse-prevention treatment strategies with sexual offenders enabled therapists to make progress with particularly intractable cases. In addition, Lindsay and colleagues reported that the good lives approach made it easier to motivate sexual offenders and to encourage them to engage in the difficult process of changing entrenched maladaptive behaviors.

Importantly, though, as a theory of rehabilitation, the GLM is able to be operationalized in numerous ways, and a number of existing programs are quite consistent with its assumptions (even though they go by different names). For instance, one example of a very successful strengths-based treatment approach that utilizes approach goals within an ecological and highly individualized model is Multi-Systemic Therapy (MST) (Henggeler *et al.*, 1998). MST has emerged as one of the few effective treatments for reducing criminality and associated negative outcomes with serious young offenders, including sexual offenders (Carr, 2005). Although very resource-intense, and therefore not easy to disseminate widely, the MST approach illustrates for our purposes both the conceptual and the empirical link between goods promotion and risk management.

MST is based on a social-ecological model and conceptualizes serious antisocial behavior as multidetermined by the myriad of factors in the young person's social systems (i.e. family, peers, school and neighborhood). MST interventions are pragmatic and goal-oriented, aiming to increase responsible behavior (and decrease irresponsible behavior) by building systemic and individual capacities within the natural setting of the young person. For example, MST interventions aim to improve caregiver discipline practices; enhance family affective relations; decrease youth association with deviant peers; improve youth school or vocational performance; engage youth in pro-social recreational outlets; and develop an indigenous support network of extended family, neighbors and friends to help caregivers achieve and maintain such changes. From a risk management and goods promotion perspective, antisocial behavior is viewed as arising from a reciprocal interaction of the individual and the social environment, with a myriad of internal and systemic (external) risk factors leading to antisocial behavior. Interventions to reduce antisocial behavior therefore aim to increase the youth's capacity (internal resources/conditions) and the social system's capacity (external conditions) to help the youth achieve better outcomes (goals/goods). Better outcomes are defined as reduced recidivism but also preservation of placement within the family home (versus residential placement or incarceration) and engagement in positive educational, vocational and social activities (secondary goods).

Another example of an existing offender program that is consistent with the GLM is the Make It Work program in Victoria, Australia (Graffam, Edwards, O'Callaghan, Shinkfield, and Lavelle, 2006). The major aims of Make It Work are to support positive lifestyle change for individuals and to reduce recidivism through a combination of vocational training and a mentoring system. The emphasis is on providing alternative models of living via mentors and also to ensure that programs are tailored to individuals' particular circumstances. The interim evaluation indicates that it has been successful in achieving these aims. In brief, individuals who had been through the program had low rates of reoffending, reduced alcohol and drug problems, improved social and family relationships, stable accommodation, and improved employment prospects.

In sum, the GLM appears to function well as an integrative framework, but so far there is a paucity of specific correctional programs that have been explicitly developed with the GLM in mind. Thus, there is a definite lack of direct, compelling research evidence for GLM-inspired programs. However, this is changing rapidly and, as we write, several correctional

GLM programmes are being constructed and empirically evaluated.

OVERALL EVALUATION OF THE GLM

So, overall, how good a theory of rehabilitation is the GLM? In our view it is a relatively coherent, integrated rehabilitation approach with a clearly articulated set of fundamental assumptions and etiological commitments. Its broad value base and ecological theoretical perspective means it is able to accommodate research ideas and findings from a wide range of scientific and social science disciplines. It is also able to incorporate the three or four principles of RNR without any difficulty, suggesting that the two theories are largely compatible despite different starting assumptions and emphases.

In our view the GLM is very useful in creating a more constructive atmosphere in offender treatment and therefore helps to reduce levels of denial and offense-supportive attitudes. Intervention workers are able to utilize all the intervention strategies currently endorsed by outcome research, but in a way that saves resources (i.e. takes individual preferences and constraints seriously) and is focused on approach goals. The GLM is able to integrate the many strengths of RNR while resolving important intervention problems faced by this extremely influential model. It can speak directly to clients about matters that concern them, such as their lives and relationships, while not ignoring the legitimate safety concerns of the community. It can provide guidance for primary, secondary and tertiary correctional crime reduction strategies and, through the promise of better lives for offenders, can lead to less harmful outcomes for members of society.

7

IN SEARCH OF COMMON GROUND

In this book we have explored two different rehabilitation theories, the Risk–Need–Responsivity Model and the Good Lives Model. Each of these theories is illustrative of a particular approach to the vexing question of how best to reduce crime and to reintegrate offenders into the community. RNR is associated with a risk management approach and as such tends to regard offender welfare as of secondary interest, as a "means" to the "end" of increased community safety. By way of contrast, the GLM proposes that advancing offenders' needs will also reduce risk. A helpful way of explaining the major difference in orientation between the RNR model and the GLM is that, while the former focuses on the deficits in the conditions necessary to achieve human goods (i.e., what is lacking and problematic), the latter is concerned with providing the conditions to obtain them. In this sense, it has a twin focus of goods promotion and capability building. These differences between the two types of rehabilitation programs ultimately reside in their overarching assumptions about the aims and nature of treatment and the general causes of crime.

However, despite these differences, there are considerable

areas of overlap, and it is possible to achieve both risk reduction and well-being enhancement by the delivery of carefully designed interventions. In the course of this book we have described and comprehensively evaluated each theory and documented its strengths and weaknesses. In our view it is reasonable to conclude the following: RNR is strongest where the GLM is weakest, and RNR is weakest where the GLM is strongest. Thus, while the (reconstructed) RNR has a narrow set of aims and struggles with issues of motivation and identity, it has an impressive research foundation. Whereas the GLM is relatively new and therefore lacks a substantial research base. Yet it is arguably a more comprehensive rehabilitation theory and is able to equip correctional workers more effectively with the tools required to motivate change. What we are left with is two overlapping but distinct rehabilitation theories with contrasting views on the nature of risk, the aims of reintegration, what generally causes crime, and how best to intervene in the lives of those on the margins of society.

Where do we go from here? One option is to adjudicate in favor of one theory and then devote our subsequent discussion to its implications for researchers, policy-makers and practitioners. Another possibility is to sidestep the debate slightly and consider what RNR and the GLM can both offer correctional workers without advocating one rather than the other. After seriously considering both alternatives, we have opted for the latter strategy. We think it is best to focus on the strengths of both approaches and thus avoid premature closure on the possibilities of either. This means taking seriously the proposal that the rehabilitation of offenders is both an *evaluative* and *capacity building* process.

We have argued that in order for an individual to be able successfully to desist from further crimes it is necessary to acquire a better sense of what activities and experiences are truly of value and equip him or her with the capabilities to secure these values in personally meaningful and socially appropriate ways. The claim is that values are objective in the sense that some kinds of experience (and activity, state of affairs, etc.) really do benefit individuals and meet their interests while others are harmful and frustrate them. Additionally, values guide all human actions and serve to orient people to what is appropriate/inappropriate, good/bad, right/wrong, helpful/unhelpful, and so on. Values and their associated commitments give people a sense of direction and purpose, and represent the terminal ends of actions and, in a more fundamental sense, lifeplans. The *evaluative* aspect of rehabilitation involves reorienting offenders to pursue primary goods in more adaptive ways and to identify those goods that are constitutive of their narrative identity. The ability to make better practical judgments, and to formulate and implement life plans that embody values and the practices associated with them, ought to be a major focus of reintegration efforts. The *capacity* or capability aspect of rehabilitation directly involves providing individuals with the internal and external conditions necessary to attain valued outcomes in ways that match their abilities, preferences and environments. Internal conditions refer to psychological characteristics such as skills, beliefs and attitudes, while external conditions refer to social resources, opportunities and supports. As stated earlier in the book, these conditions can usefully be construed as instrumental goods and their absence or distortion as criminogenic needs. What has been missing in previous discussions on rehabilitation and in RNR itself is an explicit acknowledgment of the pivotal role of values and the resources required to secure them in the reintegration process. Furthermore, the link between values (i.e., goods) and narrative identity has rarely been analyzed or debated in contemporary, mainstream RNR-derived programs.

FINAL THOUGHTS

We have been both delighted and dismayed by the current trends in correctional policy and fully appreciate the ambiguity of the old salutation/curse, "May you live in interesting times". These are indeed interesting times for researchers and practitioners working in the area of rehabilitation, and it is apparent that different cross-currents are at play. On the one hand, we are living in the heyday of "evidence-based" practice, with an impressive body of research testifying to the utility of reintegration efforts with individuals who have committed crimes. On the other hand, communities are apparently becoming more risk-aversive and punitive in their attitudes toward offenders. There appears to be a hardening of feelings and a determination to make individuals pay severely for transgressions against the state and the community (Garland, 2001). It is indeed a confusing, exhilarating and deeply worrying period in correctional history.

Perhaps most confused of all are those persons participating in the rehabilitation programming at the coalface. What must probationers, prisoners and correctional staff make of all the mixed messages they are receiving? We have tried, in this book, to ensure that our suggestions have a basis in sound theory and research and also resonate with the experiences of these correctional workers and their clients. In our opinion, if theory does not help such rehabilitation participants deal effectively with day-to-day problems, it is of little use. In this sense, we are pragmatists, albeit ones with a strong appreciation of ideas and their value as tools for changing the lives of offenders and their families.

The politics of rehabilitation since at least Martinson's moment in 1974 has been brutal, to say the least (Martinson, 1974). As Cullen (2005) reminds us, "The legitimacy once enjoyed by the treatment paradigm is shaky and must constantly be reinforced" (p. 347). In this regard, no group of researchers and theorists have done as much as the RNR proponents to convince policy-makers, the public and treatment-providers that "something works". They have raised the levels of optimism around rehabilitation no end (indeed, sometimes to the point of dangerously high expectations; see Marlowe, 2006).

Yet there is another group that needs to be convinced of the legitimacy of rehabilitation: the fellow human travelers that are labelled "offenders". They are not powerful. They are not popular. They do not pass laws or sentence people to prison (indeed, many cannot vote or even serve on juries). Yet, without their support, no one will ever save rehabilitation.

NOTES

CHAPTER 1

1 Indeed, rebranding has become a favorite sport in criminal justice departments around the world in recent years. In the UK, community service orders are now officially to be called "community punishment orders" (although judges and clients frequently still call them by their more familiar name). Prisons and probation services are now said to be in the business of "offender management." The two systems have been combined and rebranded under the bizarre acronym NOMS (or the National Offender Management Service), provoking numerous jokes about garden gnomes and one claim that the New Penology fear of prisons performing a "waste management" function had come to fruition (Padfield and Maruna, 2006).

2 This book will not feature the voices of prisoners and probationers themselves (for this, consult almost any of the authors' previous publications).

3 Such individuals also dislike the label "offenders" – as this term implies a present-tense status as well as referring to something that happened in the past (see Richards and Jones, 2004). We do our best throughout the book to avoid using this term but do not always succeed.

CHAPTER 2

1 Instead, Lynch argues, "The most suitable approach to producing knowledge about successful reentry is to describe the process of reentry that is naturally occurring" (p. 408; see also Maruna, 2001; Maruna, Immarigeon and LeBel, 2004).

CHAPTER 6

1 A percentage of this chapter is reprinted from *Aggression and Violent Behavior*, II, T. Ward and T. Gannon, "Rehabilitation, etiology, and self-regulation" pp. 77–94, (2006), with permission from Elsevier.

REFERENCES

Ackerman, S., and Hilsenroth, M. (2003). A review of therapist characteristics and techniques positively impacting the therapeutic alliance.
Clinical Psychology Review, 23, 1–33.

Akers, R. L. (1998). *Social Learning and Social Structure: A General
Theory of Crime and Deviance.* Boston, Mass.: Northeastern University
Press.

Amodeo, M., Kurtz, N., and Cutter, H. S. G. (1992). Abstinence, reasons for
not drinking, and life satisfaction. *International Journal of the Addictions,
27*, 707–16.

Andrews, D. (1995). The psychology of criminal conduct and effective
treatment. In J. McGuire (ed.), *What Works: Reducing Reoffending.*
Chichester: John Wiley.

Andrews, D. A. (2001). Principles of effective correctional programs.
In L. L. Motiuk and R. C. Serin (eds), *Compendium 2000 on Effective
Correctional Programming.* Volume 1. Canada: Ministry of Supply Services.

Andrews, D. A. (in press). Enhancing adherence to risk-need-responsivity:
Making quality a matter of policy. *Criminology and Public Policy.*

Andrews, D. A., and Bonta, J. (1995). *The Level of Service Inventory – Revised.*
Toronto: Multi-Health Systems.

Andrews, D. A., and Bonta, J. (1998). *The Psychology of Criminal Conduct,*
2nd edn. Cincinnati, Ohio: Anderson.

Andrews, D. A., and Bonta, J. (2003). *The Psychology of Criminal Conduct,*
3rd edn. Cincinnati, Ohio: Anderson.

Andrews, D. A., Bonta, J., and Hoge, R. D. (1990). Classification for
effective rehabilitation: Rediscovering psychology. *Criminal Justice and
Behavior, 17*, 19–52.

Andrews, D. A., Bonta, J., and Wormith, J. S. (2006). The recent past and near future of risk and/or need assessment. *Crime & Delinquency*, 52, 7–27.

Andrews, D. A., and Dowden, C. (2005). Managing correctional treatment for reduced recidivism: A meta-analytic review of programme integrity. *Legal and Criminological Psychology*, 10, 173–87.

Andrews, D. A., and Dowden, C. (2006). Risk principle of case classification in correctional treatment. *International Journal of Offender Therapy and Comparative Criminology*, 50, 88–100.

Andrews, D. A., Zinger, I., Hoge, R. D., Bonta, J., Gendreau, P. and Cullen, F. T. (1990). Does correctional treatment work? A clinically relevant and psychologically informed meta-analysis. *Criminology*, 28, 369–404.

Antonowicz, D. H. (2005). The Reasoning and Rehabilitation program: Outcome evaluations with offenders. In M. McMurran and J. McGuire (eds), *Social Problem Solving and Offending: Evidence, Evaluation, and Evolution*. Chichester: John Wiley.

Archer, M. S. (2000). *Being Human: The Problem of Agency*. Cambridge: Cambridge University Press.

Arnhart, L. (1998). *Darwinian Natural Right: The Biological Ethics of Human Nature*. Albany, NY: State University of New York Press.

Ashford, J. B., Sales, B. D., and Reid, W. H. (2001). *Treating Adult and Juvenile Offenders with Special Needs*. Washington, DC: American Psychological Association.

Aspinwall, L. G., and Staudinger, U. M. (2003) (eds). *A Psychology of Human Strengths: Fundamental Questions and Future Directions for a Positive Psychology*. Washington, DC: American Psychological Association.

Austin, J. (2001). Prisoner re-entry: Current trends, practices, and issues. *Crime and Delinquency*, 47, 314–34.

Austin, J. T., and Vancouver, J. B. (1996). Goal constructs in psychology: Structure, process, and content. *Psychological Bulletin*, 120, 338–75.

Bakan, D. (1966). *The Duality of Human Existence: Isolation and Communion in Western Man*. Boston, Mass.: Beacon Press.

Barry, M. (2006). *Youth Offending in Transition*. London: Routledge.

Bauer, J. J., McAdams, D. P., and Sakaeda, A. R. (2005). Interpreting the good life: Growth memories in the lives of mature, happy people. *Journal of Personality and Social Psychology*, 88, 203–17.

Baumeister, R. F. (1999) (ed.). *The Self in Social Psychology*. Philadelphia, Pa: Psychology Press.

Baumeister, R. F., and Heatherton, T. F. (1996). Self-regulation failure: An overview. *Psychological Inquiry*, 7, 1–15.

Bazemore, G. (2004). Reintegration and restorative justice: Toward a theory and practice of informal social control and support. In S. Maruna and R. Immarigeon (eds), *After Crime and Punishment*. Cullompton: Willan.

Beck, U. (1992). *Risk Society: Towards a New Modernity*. London: Sage.

Beech, A. R., and Ward, T. (2004). The integration of etiology and risk in sex offenders: A theoretical model. *Aggression and Violent Behavior, 10,* 31–63.

Birgden, A. (2004). Therapeutic jurisprudence and responsivity: Finding the will and the way in offender rehabilitation. *Crime and Law, 10*(3), 283–95.

Blackburn, R. (2000). Risk assessment and prediction. In J. McGuire, T. Mason, and A. O'Kane (eds), *Behavior, Crime and Legal Processes: A Guide for Legal Practitioners.* Chichester: John Wiley.

Blumstein, A., and Cohen, J. (1987). Characterizing criminal careers. *Science, 237,* 985–91.

Bonta, J. (1995). The responsivity principle and offender rehabilitation. *Forum on Corrections Research, 7,* 34–7.

Bonta, J. (2000). Offender assessment: general issues and considerations. *Forum on Corrections Research, 12*(2), 14–18.

Bonta, J. (2002). Offender risk assessment: Guidelines for selection and use. *Criminal Justice and Behavior, 29,* 355–79.

Bonta, J. (Personal Communication) (2003). Melbourne, Australia.

Bonta, J., and Andrews, D. A. (2003). A commentary on Ward and Stewart's model of human needs. *Psychology, Crime & Law, 9,* 215–18.

Bottoms, A. (2000). Compliance and community penalties. In A. Bottoms, L. Gelsthorpe and S. Rex (eds), *Community Penalties: Change and Challenges.* Cullompton: Willan.

Bottoms, A. E., and McWilliams, W. (1979). A non-treatment paradigm for probation practice. *British Journal of Social Work, 9*(2), 159–202.

Braithwaite, J. (1989). *Crime, Shame and Reintegration.* Cambridge: Cambridge University Press.

Braithwaite, J., and Braithwaite, V. (2001). "Part One." In E. Ahmed, N. Harris, J. Braithwaite and V. Braithwaite (eds), *Shame Management through Reintegration.* Cambridge: University of Cambridge Press.

Braithwaite, J., and Roche, D. (2001). Responsibility and restorative justice. In G. Bazemore and M. Schiff (eds), *Restorative Community Justice: Repairing Harm and Transforming Communities.* Cincinnati, Ohio: Anderson.

Brandtstadter, J. (1999). The self in action and development: Cultural, biosocial, and ontogenetic bases of intentional self-development. In J. Brandtstadter and R. M. Lerner (eds), *Action and Self-development: Theory and Research through the Life Span.* Thousand Oaks, Calif.: Sage.

Braybrooke, D. (1987). *Meeting Needs.* Princeton, NJ: Princeton University Press.

Brerscheid, E. (2003). The human's greatest strength: Other humans. In L. G. Aspinwall and U. M. Staudinger (eds), *A Psychology of Human Strengths: Fundamental Questions and Future Directions for a Positive Psychology.* Washington, DC: American Psychological Association.

Bronfenbrenner, U. (1979). *The Ecology of Human Development: Experiments by Nature and Design*. Cambridge, Mass.: Harvard University Press.

Brown, M. (2000). Calculations of risk in contemporary penal practice. In M. Brown and J. Pratt (eds), *Dangerous Offenders: Punishment and Social Order*. London: Routledge.

Bruner, J. (1986). *Actual Minds, Possible Worlds*. Cambridge, Mass.: Harvard University Press.

Bruner, J. (1990). *Acts of Meaning*. Cambridge, Mass.: Harvard University Press.

Buller, D. J., and Hardcastle, V. G. (2000). Evolutionary psychology meets developmental neurobiology: Against promiscuous modularity. *Brain and Mind*, 1, 307–25.

Bumby, K. M., and Hansen, D. J. (1997). Intimacy deficits, fear of intimacy, and loneliness among sexual offenders. *Criminal Justice and Behavior*, 24(3), 315–31.

Burgess, A. (1962). *A Clockwork Orange*. New York: Norton.

Burnett, R. (2004). To re-offend or not to re-offend? The ambivalence of convicted property offenders. In S. Maruna and R. Immarigeon (eds), *After Crime and Punishment: Pathways to Desistance from Crime*. Cullompton: Willan.

Burnett, R., and Maruna, S. (2006). The kindness of prisoners: Strength-based resettlement in theory and in action. *Criminology and Criminal Justice*, 6, 83–106.

Cafaro, P. (2006). *Thoreau's Living Ethics: Walden and the Pursuit of Virtue*. Athens, Ga: University of Georgia Press.

Cann, J., Falshaw, L., Nugent, F., and Friendship, C. (2003). *Understanding What Works: Accredited Cognitive Skills Programmes for Adult Men and Young Offenders*. Home Office Research Findings No. 226. London: Home Office.

Capaldi, Deborah M. (1992). Co-occurrence of conduct problems and depressive symptoms in early adolescent boys: II. A 2-year follow-up at grade 8. *Development and Psychopathology 4*, 125–44.

Carlen, P. (1994). Crime, inequality and sentencing. In A. Duff and D. Garland (eds), *A Reader on Punishment*. Oxford: Oxford University Press.

Carr, A. (2005). Contributions to the study of violence and trauma: Multisystemic therapy, exposure therapy, attachment styles, and therapy process research. *Journal of Interpersonal Violence*, 20, 426–35.

Carroll, K. M. (1998). *Therapy Manuals for Drug Addiction: A Cognitive-behavioral Approach – treating cocaine addiction*. National Institute of Health Publication #98–4308. Washington, DC: US Department of Health and Human Services.

Cassandro, V. J., and Simonton, D. K. (2003). Creativity and genius. In C. L. M. Keyes and J. Haidt (eds), *Flourishing: Positive Psychology and the Life Well-lived*. Washington, DC: American Psychological Association.

Chen, H. (1990). *Theory-driven Evaluation*. Newbury Park, Calif.: Sage.

Chiles, J., Miller, M., and Cox, G. (1980). Depression in an adolescent delinquent population. *Archives of General Psychiatry*, *37*, 1179–84.

Christian Science Monitor (2005). California turns toward rehabilitating juveniles, 27 May.

Chui, W. H., and Nellis, M. (2003) (eds). *Moving Probation Forward: Evidence, Arguments and Practice*. Harlow: Pearson Education.

Clark, A. (2003). *Natural-born Cyborgs: Minds, Technologies, and the Future of Human Intelligence*. New York: Oxford University Press.

Cohen, J. (1988). *Statistical power analysis for the behavioral sciences* (2nd ed.). Hillsdale, NJ: Lawrence Earlbaum Associates.

Cohen, Stanley (1985). *Visions of Social Control: Crime, Punishment, and Classification*. Cambridge: Polity.

Cressey, D. R. (1958). The nature and effectiveness of correctional techniques. *Law and Contemporary Problems*, *23*(4), 754–71.

Crow, I. (2001). *The treatment and Rehabilitation of Offenders*. Thousand Oaks, Calif.: Sage.

Cullen, F. (2005). The twelve people who saved rehabilitation: How the science of criminology made a difference. *Criminology*, *43*(1), 1–42.

Cullen, F., and Gendreau, P. (2000). Assessing correctional rehabilitation: Policy, practice, and prospects. *Criminal Justice*, *3*, 109–75.

Cullen, F., and Gilbert, K. E. (1982). *Reaffirming Rehabilitation*. Cincinnati, Ohio: Anderson.

Cullen, F. T. (2002) Rehabilitation and treatment programs. In J. Q. Wilson and J. Petersilia (eds), *Crime: Public Policies for Crime Control*. Oakland, Calif.: Institute for Contemporary Studies.

Cummins, R. A. (1996). The domains of life satisfaction: An attempt to order chaos. *Social Indicators Research*, *38*, 303–28.

D'Andrade, R. (1995). *The Development of Cognitive Anthropology*. Cambridge: Cambridge University Press.

De Coster, Stacy, and Heimer, Karen (2001). The relationship between law violation and depression: An interactionist analysis. *Criminology*, *39*, 799–836.

Deci, E. L., and Ryan, R. M. (2000). The "what" and "why" of goal pursuits: Human needs and the self-determination of behavior. *Psychological Inquiry*, *11*, 227–68.

Denny, D. (2005). *Risk and Society*. London: Sage.

Diener, E. (2000). Subjective well-being: The science of happiness and a proposal for a national index. *American Psychologist*, *55*(1), 34–43.

Diener, E., Emmons, R. A., Larson, R. J., and Griffin, S. (1999). Subjective well-being: Three decades of progress. *Psychological Bulletin*, *125*(2), 276–302.

Dobransky, P. (1999). *Mind OS: How the "Operating System of the Human Mind" Is the Ultimate Solution to Every Personal or Business Problem*. Unpublished manuscript, Denver, Colo.

Douglas, M. (1985). *Risk Acceptability According to the Social Sciences*. New York: Russell Sage Foundation.

Douglas, M. (1992). *Risk and Blame*. London: Routledge.

Dowden, C., and Andrews, D. A. (1999a). What works in young offender treatment: a meta-analysis. *Forum on Corrections Research, 11*, 21–4.

Dowden, C., and Andrews, D. A. (1999b). What works for female offenders: a meta-analytic review. *Crime and Delinquency, 45*, 438–52.

Dowden, C., and Andrews, D. A. (2000). Effective correctional treatment and violent reoffending: A meta-analysis. *Canadian Journal of Criminology and Criminal Justice, 42*, 449–67.

Dowden, C., and Andrews, D. A. (2003). Does family intervention work for delinquents? Results of a meta-analysis. *Canadian Journal of Criminology and Criminal Justice, 45*, 327–42.

Dowden, C., and Andrews, D. A. (2004). The importance of staff practice in delivering effective correctional treatment: A meta-analytic review of core correctional practice. *International Journal of Offender Therapy and Comparative Criminology, 48*, 203–14.

Dowden, C., Antonowicz, D., and Andrews, D. A. (2003). The effectiveness of relapse prevention with offenders: A meta-analysis. *International Journal of Offender Therapy and Comparative Criminology, 47*, 516–28.

Draine, J., Wolff, N., Jacoby, J. E., Hartwell, S., and Duclos, C. (2006). Understanding community re-entry of former prisoners with mental illness: A conceptual model to guide new research. *Behavioral Sciences and the Law, 5*, 689–707.

Duguid, S. (2000). *Can Prisons Work? The Prisoner as Object and Subject in Modern Corrections*. Toronto: University of Toronto Press.

Ellerby, L., Bedard, J., and Chartrand, S. (2000). Holism, wellness and spirituality. In D. R. Laws, S. M. Hudson and T. Ward (eds), *Remaking Relapse Prevention with Sex Offenders*. Newbury Park, Calif.: Sage.

Emmons, R. (1986). Personal strivings: An approach to personality and subjective well-being. *Journal of Personality and Social Psychology, 51*, 1058–68.

Emmons, R. A. (1996). Striving and feeling: Personal goals and subjective well-being. In P. M. Gollwitzer and J. A. Bargh (eds). *The Psychology of Action: Linking Cognition and Motivation to Behavior*. New York: Guilford.

Emmons, R. A. (1999). *The Psychology of Ultimate Concerns*. New York: Guilford.

Emmons, R. A. (2003). Personal goals, life meaning, and virtue: well-springs of a positive life. In C. L. M. Keyes and J. Haidt (eds), *Flourishing: Positive Psychology and the Life Well-lived*. Washington, DC: American Psychological Association.

Fabiano, E., and Porporino, F. (2002). *Focus on Resettlement – a Change*. Canada: T3 Associates.

Falshaw, L., Friendship, C., Travers, R., and Nugent, F. (2003). *Searching for*

"What Works": An Evaluation of Cognitive Skills Programmes. Home Office Research Findings No. 26. London: Home Office.

Farabee, D. (2005). Rethinking Rehabilitation: Why Can't We Reform Our Criminals?. Washington, DC: American Enterprise Institute Press.

Farrall, S. (1995). Why do people stop offending? Scottish Journal of Criminal Justice Studies, 1, 51–9.

Farrall, S. (2004). Social capital and offender reintegration: Making probation desistance focussed. In S. Maruna and R. Immarigeon (eds), After Crime and Punishment: Pathways to Offender Reintegration. Cullompton: Willan.

Farrall, S., and Calverley, A. (2006). Understanding Desistance from Crime: Theoretical Directions in Resettlement and Rehabilitation. Maidenhead: Open University Press.

Farrant, F. (2006). Out for Good: The Resettlement Needs of Young Men in Prison. London: Howard League for Penal Reform.

Feeley, M. M., and Simon, J. (1992). The new penology: Notes on the emerging strategy of corrections and its implications. Criminology, 30, 449–74.

Gable, S. L. (2006). Approach and avoidance social motives and goals. Journal of Personality, 74, 175–222.

Gaes, G. G., Flanagan, T. J., Motiuk, L. L., and Stewart, L. (1999). Adult correctional treatment. Crime and Justice: A Review of Research, 26, 361–426.

Garland, D. (2001). The Culture of Control: Crime and Social Order in Contemporary Society. Chicago, Ill.: University of Chicago Press.

Geary, B. (2002). The Contribution of Spirituality to Well-being in Sex Offenders. Unpublished doctoral thesis, Loyola College, Maryland.

Gecas, V., and Schwalbe, M. L. (1983). Beyond the looking-glass self: Social structure and efficacy-based self-esteem. Social Psychology Quarterly, 46(2), 77–88.

Gendreau, P. (1981). Treatment in corrections: Martinson was wrong. Canadian Psychology, 22, 332–8.

Gendreau, P., and Andrews, D. A. (1990). Tertiary prevention: What a meta-analysis of the offender treatment literature tells us about "what works". Canadian Journal of Criminology, 32, 173–84.

Gendreau, P., Little, T., and Goggin, C. (1996). A meta-analysis of the predictors of adult offender recidivism: What works! Criminology, 34, 575–607.

Gendreau, P., Goggin, C., Cullen, F. T., and Andrews, D. A. (2000). The effects of community sanctions and incarceration on recidivism. In L. L. Motiuk and R. C. Serin (eds), Compendium 2000 on Effective Correctional Programming. Ottawa: Correctional Services Canada.

Gendreau, P., Goggin, C., and Smith, P. (2002). Is the PCL-R really the "unparalleled" measure of offender risk? A lesson in knowledge cumulation. Criminal Justice and Behavior, 29, 397–426.

Gillis, C. A. (2000). Offender Employment Programming. In L. L. Motiuk and R. C. Serin (eds), *Compendium 2000 on Effective Correctional Programming*. Retrieved 26 March 2006 from http://www.csc-scc.gc.ca/text/rsrch/compendium/2000/index_e.shtml

Giordano, P. C., Cernkovich, S. A., and Rudolph, J. L. (2002). Gender, crime and desistance: Toward a theory of cognitive transformation. *American Journal of Sociology, 107*, 990–1064.

Gottfredson, M., and Hirschi, T. (1990). *A General Theory of Crime*. Stanford, Calif: Stanford University Press.

Gottfredson, M. R. (1979). Parole guidelines and reduction of sentence disparity. *Journal of Research on Crime and Delinquency, 16*, 218–31.

Gottfredson, P., and Taylor, R. (1988). Community contexts and criminal offenders. In T. Hop and M. Shaw (eds), *Community and Crime Reduction*. London: Her Majesty's Stationery Office.

Graffam, J., Edwards, D., O'Callaghan, P., Shinkfield, A., and Lavelle, B. (2006). *Make It Work. An Employment Assistance and Mentoring Program for Offenders: A Comprehensive Evaluation*. Melbourne: Deakin University.

Green, R. (1995). Psycho-educational modules. In B. K. Schwartz and H. R. Cellini (eds), *The Sex Offender: Corrections, Treatment, and Legal Practice*, Vol. 1. Kingston, NJ: Civic Research Institute.

Griffin, J. (1996). *Value Judgement: Improving Our Ethical Beliefs*. New York: Oxford University Press.

Grove, W. M., Zald, D. H., Lebow, B. S., Snitz, B. E., and Nelson, C. (2000). Clinical versus mechanical prediction: A meta-analysis. *Psychological Assessment, 12*, 19–30.

Haaven, J. L., and Coleman, E. M. (2000). Treatment of the developmentally disabled sex offender. In D. R. Laws, S. M. Hudson and T. Ward (eds), *Remaking Relapse Prevention with Sex Offenders: A Sourcebook*. Thousand Oaks, Calif: Sage.

Halsey, M. (2006). Negotiating conditional release: Juvenile narratives of repeat incarceration. *Punishment and Society, 8*, 147–81.

Hannah-Moffat, K. (1999). Moral agent or actuarial subject: Risk and women's imprisonment. *Theoretical Criminology, 3*, 71–94.

Hannah-Moffat, K. (2005). Criminogenic needs and the transformative risk subject. *Punishment and Society, 7*(1), 29–51.

Hanson, R., Gordon, A., Harris, A., Marques, J., Murphy, W., Quinsey, V., and Seto, M. (2002). First report of the collaborative outcome data project on the effectiveness of psychological treatment for sex offenders. *Sexual Abuse: Journal of Research and Treatment, 14*, 169–94.

Hanson, R. K. (2001). *Age and Sexual Recidivism: A Comparison of Rapists and Child Molesters*. Ottawa: Solicitor General Canada.

Hanson, R. K., and Morton-Bourgon, K. E. (2005). The characteristics of persistent sexual offenders: A meta-analysis of recidivism studies. *Journal of Consulting and Clinical Psychology, 73*, 1154–63.

Harris, M. K. (2005). In search of common ground: The importance of theoretical orientations in criminology and criminal justice. *Criminology and Public Policy*, *4*, 311–28.

Helson, R., and Stewart, A. (1994). Personality change in adulthood. In T. F. Heatherton and J. L. Weinberger (eds), *Can Personality Change?* Washington, DC: American Psychological Association.

Henggeler, S. W., Schoenwald, S. K., Borduin, C. M., Rowland, M. D., and Cunningham, P. B. (1998). *Multisystemic Treatment of Antisocial Behavior in Children and Adolescents*. New York: Guilford.

Hillman, J., and Ventura, M. (1993). *We've Had a Hundred Years of Psychotherapy – and the World's Getting Worse*. San Francisco, Calif.: Harper.

Hoffman, P. B., and Beck, J. L. (1974). Parole decision-making: a salient factor score. *Journal of Criminal Justice*, *2*, 195–206.

Hoffman, P. B., and Beck, J. L. (1985). Recidivism among released federal prisoners: Salient factor score and five-year follow-up. *Criminal Justice and Behavior*, *12*, 501–7.

Hollin, C. R. (1999). Treatment programs for offenders: Meta-analysis, "what works" and beyond. *International Journal of Law and Psychiatry*, *22*, 361–72.

Hooker, C. A. (1987). *A Realistic Theory of Science*. New York: State University of New York Press.

Horvath, A. O., and Luborsky, L. (1993). The role of the therapeutic alliance in psychotherapy. *Journal of Consulting and Clinical Psychology*, *61*, 561–73.

Ignatieff, M. (1984). *The Needs of Strangers*. Harmondsworth: Penguin.

Irwin, John (1974). The trouble with rehabilitation. *Criminal Justice and Behavior*, *1*(2), 139–49.

Jenkins, P. (1998). *Moral Panic: Changing Concepts of the Child Molester in Modern America*. Boston, Mass.: Yale University Press.

Jorgensen, I. S., and Nafstad, H. E. (2004). Positive psychology: Historical, philosophical, and epistemological perspectives. In P. A. Linley and S. Joseph (eds), *Positive Psychology in Practice*. New York: John Wiley.

Kekes, J. (1989). *Moral Tradition and Individuality*. Princeton, NJ: Princeton University Press.

Kekes, J. (1993). *The Morality of Pluralism*. Princeton, NJ: Princeton University Press.

Kelly, W. E. (2003). Some correlates of sleep disturbance ascribed to worry. *Individual Differences Research*, *1*(2), 137–46.

Kelman, Herbert C. (1958). Compliance, identification and internalization: Three processes of opinion change. *Journal of Conflict Resolution*, *2*, 51–60.

King, L. A. (2001). The hard road to the Good Life: The happy, mature person. *Journal of Humanistic Psychology*, *41*(1), 51–72.

King, L. A., Eells J. A., and Burton, C. M. (2004). The good life, broadly defined. In P. A. Linley and S. Joseph (eds), *Positive psychology in practice*. New Jersey: John Wiley.

Kitcher, P. (2001). *Science, Truth, and Democracy*. New York: Oxford University Press.

Korn, R. (1992). Novum Organum: An argument for a fundamentally different curriculum in criminal justice. *The Criminologist*, 17(2), 1–7.

Kruttschnitt, C., Uggen, C., and Shelton, K. (2000). Predictors of desistance among sex offenders: The interaction of formal and informal social controls. *Justice Quarterly*, 17(1), 61–87.

Kukla, A. (2001). *Methods of Theoretical Psychology*. Cambridge, Mass.: MIT Press.

Kyvsgaard, B. (1991). The living conditions of law violators in Denmark. *International Journal of Offender Therapy and Comparative Criminology*, 35(3), 235–47.

Latimer, J. (2001). A meta-analytic examination of youth delinquency, family treatment, and recidivism. *Canadian Journal of Criminology*, 43, 237–253.

Laub, J. H., Nagin, D. S., and Sampson, R. J. (1998). Trajectories of change in criminal offending: Good marriages and the desistance process. *American Sociological Review*, 63(2), 225–38.

Laub, John H., and Sampson, Robert J. (2001). Understanding desistance from crime. In M. Tonry (ed.), *Crime and Justice: A Review of Research*, vol. 28. Chicago, Ill: University of Chicago Press.

Laws, D. R., Hudson, S. M., and Ward, T. (2000) (eds). *Remaking Relapse Prevention with Sex Offenders*. Thousand Oaks, Calif.: Sage Publications.

Lewis, S. (2005) Rehabilitation: Headline or footnote in the new penal policy? *Probation Journal*, 52(2), 119–36.

Lewis, S., Vennard, J., Maguire, M., Raynor, P., Vanstone, M., Raybould, S., and Rix, A. (2003). *The Resettlement of Short-Term Prisoners: An Evaluation of Seven Pathfinders*, RDS Occasional Paper 83. London: Home Office.

Liebling, A., and Maruna, S. (2005) (eds). *The Effects of Imprisonment*. Cullompton: Willan.

Liebmann, M. (1994). Art therapy and changing probation values. In M. Liebmann (ed.), *Art Therapy with Offenders*. Philadelphia, Pa: Jessica Kingsley.

Lin, A. C. (2000). *Reform in the Making: The Implementation of Social Policy in Prison*. Princeton, NJ: Princeton University Press.

Lindsay, W. R., Ward, T., Morgan, T., and Wilson. I. (2006). *Self-regulation of Sex Offending, Future Pathways and the Good Lives Model: Applications and Problems*. Manuscript under review.

Linley, P. A., and Joseph, S. (2004). Applied positive psychology: A new perspective for professional practice. In P. A. Linley and S. Joseph (eds), *Positive Psychology in Practice*. New York: John Wiley.

Lippke, R. (2003). Diminished opportunities, diminished capacities: Social deprivation and punishment. *Social Theory and Practice*, 29(3), 459–85.

Lipsey, M., and Wilson, D. (2002). Effective intervention for serious juvenile offenders: A synthesis of research. In R. Leober and D. Farrington (eds), *Serious and Violent Juvenile Offenders: Risk Factors and Successful Interventions*. Thousands Oaks, Calif.: Sage Publications.

Lipsey, M. W. (1992). Juvenile delinquency treatment: A meta-analytic inquiry into the variability of effects. In T. D. Cook, H. Cooper, D. S. Cordray, H. Hartmann, L. V. Hedges, R. J. Light, T. A. Louis, and F. Mosteller (eds), *Meta-Analysis for Explanation: A Casebook*. New York: Russell Sage Foundation.

Lipsey, M. W., Chapman, G. L., and Landenberger, N. A. (2001). Cognitive-behavioral programs for offenders. *The ANNALS of the American Academy of Political and Social Science*, 578(1), 144–57.

Logan, C. H., and Gaes, G. G. (1993). Meta-analysis and the rehabilitation of punishment. *Justice Quarterly* 10(2), 245–63.

Lösel, F. (1995). What recent meta-evaluations tell us about the effectiveness of correctional treatment. In G. Davies, S. Loyd-Bostock, M. McMurran and C. Wilson (eds), *Psychology, Law and Criminal Justice: International Developments in Research and Practice*, 537–54.

Lowenkamp, C., Latessa, E., and Holsinger, A. (2006). The risk principle in action: What have we learned from 13,676 offenders and 97 correctional programs? *Crime and Delinquency*, 52, 77–93.

Lutz, F. (2006). Boot camp prisons and corrections policy: Moving from militarism to an ethic of care. *Criminology and Public Policy*, 5, 389–400.

Lynch, J. P. (2006). Prisoner reentry: Beyond program evaluation. *Criminology and Public Policy*, 5, 401–12.

Lynch, J. P., and Sabol, W. J. (2001). *Prison Reentry in Perspective*. Crime Policy Report Vol. 3. Washington, DC: Urban Institute Justice Policy Center.

McAdams, D. P. (1985) *Power, Intimacy and the Life Story: Personological Inquiries into Identity*. New York: Guilford Press.

McAdams, D. P. (1994). Can personality change? Levels of stability and growth in personality across the life span. In T. F. Heatherton and J. L. Weinberger (eds), *Can Personality Change?* Washington, DC: American Psychological Association.

McAdams, D. P. (2006). *The Redemptive Self: Stories Americans Live By*. New York: Oxford.

McAdams, D. P., Hoffman, B. J., Mansfield, E. D., and Day, R. (1996). Themes of agency and communion in significant autobiographical scenes. *Journal of Personality*, 64, 339–77.

McCord, J. (2003). Cures that harm: Unanticipated outcomes of crime prevention programs. *Annals of the American Academy of Political and Social Science*, 587, 16–30.

McCulloch, P. (2005). Probation, social context and desistance: Retracing the relationship. *Probation Journal*, 52, 8–22.

McGuire, J. (2000). Explanations of criminal behavior. In J. McGuire, T. Mason and A. O'Kane (eds), *Behavior, Crime and Legal Processes: A Guide for Legal Practitioners*. Chichester: John Wiley.

McGuire, J. (2002). Criminal sanctions versus psychologically-based interventions with offenders: A comparative empirical analysis. *Psychology, Crime, and Law, 8*, 183–208.

McGuire, J. (2004). *Understanding Psychology and Crime: Perspectives on Theory and Action.* Maidenhead: Open University Press.

MacKenzie, D. L. (2006). *What Works in Corrections: Reducing the Recidivism of Offenders and Delinquents.* Cambridge: Cambridge University Press.

MacKenzie, D., Wilson, D., and Kider, S. (2001). Effects of correctional boot camps on offending. *Annals of the American Academy of Political and Social Science, 578*, 126–43.

McLeod, Jane D., and Shanahan, Michael J. (1993). Poverty, parenting, and children's mental health. *American Sociological Review, 58*, 351–66.

McManus, Michael, Alessi, Norman E., Grapentine, W. Lexington, and Brickman, Arthur S. (1984). Psychiatric disturbance in serious delinquents. *Journal of the American Academy of Child Psychiatry, 23*, 602–25.

McMurran, M. (2002). *Motivating Offenders to Change.* Chichester: John Wiley.

McMurran, M., and Ward, T. (2004). Motivating offenders to change in therapy: An organizing framework. *Legal and Criminological Psychology, 9*, 295–311.

McNeill, F. (2003). Desistance-focused probation practice. In W. Hong Chui and M. Nellis (eds), *Moving Probation Forward.* Harlow: Pearson Longman.

McNeill, F. (2006). A desistance paradigm for offender management. *Criminology and Criminal Justice, 6*, 39–62.

McRae, R. R., and Costa, P. T. (1994). The stability of personality: observations and evaluations. *Current Directions in Psychological Science, 3*(6), 173–5.

Maguire, M., and Raynor, P. (2006). How the resettlement of prisoners promotes desistance from crime: Or does it? *Criminology and Criminal Justice, 6*, 19–38.

Mair, G. (2004). *What Matters in Probation.* Cullompton: Willan.

Maloney, D., Bazemore, G., and Hudson, J. (2001). The end of probation and the beginning of community justice. *Perspectives, 25*(3), 24–30.

Mann, R. E., and Shingler, J. (2006). Collaboration in clinical work with sexual offenders: Treatment and risk assessment. In W. L. Marshall, Y. M. Fernandez, L. E. Marshall and G. A. Serran (eds), *Sexual Offender Treatment: Controversial Issues.* Chichester: John Wiley.

Mann, R. E., Webster, S. D., Schofield, C., and Marshall, W. L. (2004). Approach versus avoidance goals in relapse prevention with sexual offenders. *Sexual Abuse: A Journal of Research and Treatment, 16*, 65–76.

Marlowe, D. B. (2006). When "what works" never did: Dodging the

"Scarlet M" in correctional rehabilitation. *Criminology and Public Policy*, 5, 339–47.

Marshall, W. L. (1999). Current status of North American assessment and treatment programs for sexual offenders. *Journal of Interpersonal Violence*, 14, 221–39.

Marshall, W. L., and Marshall, L. E. (2000). The origins of sexual offending. *Trauma, Violence, & Abuse*, 1, 250–63

Marshall, W. L., and Serran, G. A. (2004). The role of the therapist in offender treatment. *Psychology, Crime and Law*, 10, 309–20.

Marshall, W. L., Hudson, S. M., and Hodkinson, S. (1993). The importance of attachment bonds in the development of juvenile sex offending. In H. E. Barbaree, W. L. Marshall and S. M. Hudson (eds), *The Juvenile Sex Offender*. New York: Guilford Press.

Marshall, W. L., Anderson, D., and Fernandez, Y. (1999). *Cognitive Behavioural Treatment of Sexual Offenders*. New York: John Wiley.

Marshall, W. L., Fernandez, Y. M., Serran, G. A., Mulloy, R., Thornton, D., Mann, R. E., and Anderson, D. (2003). Process variables in the treatment of sexual offenders. *Aggression and Violent Behavior: A Review Journal*, 8, 205–234.

Marshall, W. L., Serran, G. A., Fernandez, Y. M., Mulloy, R., Mann, R. E., and Thornton, D. (2003). Therapist characteristics in the treatment of sexual offenders: Tentative data on their relationship with indices of behaviour change. *Journal of Sexual Aggression*, 9, 25–30.

Martin, P. (2005). *Making Happy People: The Nature of Happiness and Its Origins in Childhood*. London: Fourth Estate.

Martinson, R. (1974). What works? – questions and answers about prison reform. *The Public Interest*, 35, 22–54.

Martinson, R. (1976). California research at the crossroads. *Crime and Delinquency*, 22, 180–91.

Maruna, S. (2001). *Making Good: How Ex-Convicts Reform and Rebuild Their Lives*. Washington, DC: American Psychological Association.

Maruna, S. (2004). Desistance and explanatory style: A new direction in the psychology of reform. *Journal of Contemporary Criminal Justice*, 20, 184–200.

Maruna, S. (2006). Who owns resettlement? Towards restorative re-integration. *British Journal of Community Justice*, 4(2), 23–33.

Maruna, S., and LeBel, T. (2003). Welcome home?: Examining the reentry court concept from a strengths-based perspective. *Western Criminology Review*, 4(2), 91–107.

Maruna, S., and Immarigeon, R. (2004) (eds). *After Crime and Punishment: Pathways to Offender Reintegration*. Cullompton: Willan.

Maruna, S., and Mann, R. (2006). Fundamental attribution errors? Re-thinking cognitive distortions. *Legal and Criminological Psychology*, 11, 155–77.

Maruna, S., Immarigeon, R., and LeBel, T. (2004). Ex-Offender Reintegration: Theory and Practice. In S. Maruna and R. Immarigeon (eds), *After Crime and Punishment: Pathways to Ex-Offender Reintegration*. Cullompton: Willan Books.

Maruna, S., LeBel, T., Mitchel, N., and Naples, M. (2004). Pygmalion in the reintegration process: Desistance from crime through the looking glass. *Psychology, Crime and Law*, 10(3), 271–81.

Maruna, S., Porter, L., and Carvalho, I. (2004). The Liverpool desistance study and probation practice: Opening the dialogue. *Probation Journal*, 51, 221–32.

Maslow, Abraham H. (1970). *Motivation and Personality*, 2nd edn. New York: Harper & Row.

Matza, D. (1964). *Delinquency and Drift*. New York: John Wiley.

Messner, S. F., and Rosenfeld, R. (2001). *Crime and the American Dream*, 3rd edn. Belmont, Calif.: Wadsworth.

Miller, W. R., and Rollnick, S. (2002). *Motivational Interviewing: Preparing People for Change*. New York: Guilford Press.

Moffitt, T. E. (1993). Adolescence-limited and life-course-persistent anti-social behavior: A developmental taxonomy. *Psychological Review*, 100, 674–701.

Monk, G., Winslade, J., Crocket, K., and Epston, D. (1996). *Narrative Therapy in Practice: The Archaeology of Hope*. San Francisco, Calif.: Jossey-Bass.

Morgan, Rod, and Owers, Anne (2001). *Through the Prison Gate: A Joint Thematic Review by HM Inspectorates of Prisons and Probation*. London: HM Inspectorate of Prisons.

Morris, N., and Rothman, D. (1995). *The Oxford History of the Prison*. New York: Oxford University Press.

Mrazek, P. J., and Haggerty, R. J. (1994). *Reducing Risks for Mental Disorders: Frontiers for Preventive Intervention*. Washington, DC: National Academy Press.

Mulcahy, A. (2006). *Policing Northern Ireland: Conflict, Legitimacy and Reform*. Cullompton: Willan.

Murphy, M. C. (2001). *Natural Law and Practical Rationality*. New York: Cambridge University Press.

Nagin, D. S., and Paternoster, R. (1991). On the relationship of past and future participation in delinquency. *Criminology*, 29, 163–90.

Newburn, T. (2002). Atlantic crossings: policy transfer and crime control in England and Wales. *Punishment and Society*, 4, 165–94.

Newton-Smith, W. (2002). *A Companion to the Philosophy of Science*. Oxford: Blackwell.

Nussbaum, M. C. (2000). *Women and Human Development: The Capabilities approach*. New York: Cambridge University Press.

Odling-Smee, F. J., Laland, K. N., and Feldman, M. W. (2003). *Niche Construction: The Neglected Process in Evolution*. Princeton, NJ: Princeton University Press.

Ogloff, J. R. O., and Davis, M. R. (2004). Advances in offender assessment and rehabilitation: Contributions of the Risk–Needs–Responsivity approach. *Psychology, Crime & Law*, 10, 229–42.

Ouimet, M., and Le Blanc, M. (1996). The role of life experiences in the continuation of the adult criminal career. *Criminal Behaviour and Mental Health*, 6(1), 73–97.

Oyserman, D., and Markus, H. R. (1990). Possible selves and delinquency. *Journal of Personality and Social Psychology*, 59(1), 112–25.

Padfield, N., and Maruna, S. (2006). The revolving door: Exploring the rise in recalls to prison. *Criminology and Criminal Justice*, 6, 329–52.

Pallone, N. J., and Hennessy, J. J. (2003). To punish or to treat: Substance abuse within the context of oscillating attitudes toward correctional rehabilitation. *Journal of Offender Rehabilitation*, 37(3–4), 1–25.

Palmer, T. (1975). Martinson revisited. *Journal of Research in Crime and Delinquency*, 12, 133–52.

Palmer, T. (1994). *A Profile of Correctional Effectiveness and New Directions for research*. Albany, NY: State University of New York Press.

Patterson, G. R. (1993). Orderly change in a stable world: The antisocial trait as chimera. *Journal of Consulting and Clinical Psychology*, 61, 911–19.

Pawson, R., and Tilley, N. (1997). *Realistic Evaluation*. London: Sage.

Pearson, F., and Lipton, D. (1999). A meta-analytic review of the effectiveness of corrections-based treatments for drug abuse. *The Prison Journal*, 79, 384–410.

Pearson, F., Lipton, D., Cleland, C., and Yee, D. (2002). The effects of behavioral/cognitive-behavioral programs on recidivism. *Crime and Delinquency*, 48, 476–96.

Petersilia, J. (2003). *When Prisoners Come Home: Parole and Prisoner Reentry*. Oxford: Oxford University Press.

Peterson, C., and Seligman, M. E. P. (2004). *Character Strengths and Virtues: A Handbook and Classification*. New York: Oxford University Press.

Petrosino, A., Turpin-Petrosino, C., and Fincknaeuer, J. (2000). Well-meaning programs can have harmful effects! Lessons from experiments of programs such as scared straight. *Crime and Delinquency*, 46, 354–79.

Presser, L. (2004). Violent offenders, moral selves: Constructing identities and accounts in the research interview. *Social Problems*, 51, 82–101.

Prochaska, J. O., and DiClemente, C. C. (1982). Transtheoretical therapy: toward a more integrative model of change. *Psychotherapy-Theory Research and Practice*, 19(3), 276–88.

Prochaska, J. O., and DiClemente, C. C. (1998). Comments, criteria, and creating better models: In response to Davidson. In W. R. Miller and N. Heather (eds), *Treating Addictive Behaviors*, 2nd edn. New York: Plenum.

Psillos, S. (1999). *Scientific Realism: How Science Tracks Truth*. London: Routledge.

Purvis, M. (2005). *Good Lives Plans and Sexual Offending: A Preliminary Study*. Unpublished doctoral dissertation, University of Melbourne, Australia.

Raynor, P. (1985). *Social Work, Justice and Control*. New York: Blackwell.

Raynor, P., and Robinson, G. (2005). *Rehabilitation, Crime and Justice*. Basingstoke: Palgrave.

Redondo, S., Sanchez-Meca, J., and Garrido, V. (2002). Crime treatment in Europe: A review of outcome studies. In J. McGuire (ed.), *Offender Rehabilitation and Treatment: Effective Programmes and Policies to Reduce Re-offending*. New York: John Wiley.

Re-entry Policy Council (2005). *Report of the Re-entry Policy Council*. New York: Re-entry Policy Council, Council of State Governments.

Rescher, N. (1993). *A System of Pragmatic Idealism*, Vol. 2, *The Validity of Values*. Princeton, NJ: Princeton University Press.

Rex, S. (1999). Desistance from offending: Experiences of probation. *The Howard Journal, 38*, 366–83.

Rhine, E. E., Mawhorr, T. L., and Parks, E. C. (2006). Implementation: The bane of effective correctional programs. *Criminology & Public Policy, 5*, 347–58.

Richards, S. C. and Jones, R. S. (2004). Beating the perpetual incarnation machine: overcoming structural impediments to re-entry. In S. Maruna and R. Immarigeon (eds.), *After Crime and Punishment: Pathways to Offender Reintegration*. Cullompton: Willan Books.

Robinson, G. (1999). Risk management and rehabilitation in the probation service: Collision and collusion. *The Howard Journal, 38*(4), 421–33.

Rosenberg, M. (1965). The measurement of self-esteem. In *Society and the Adolescent Self-image*. Princeton, NJ: Princeton University Press.

Ross, R. R. (1995). The reasoning and rehabilitation program for high-risk probationers and prisoners. In R. R. Ross, D. H. Antonowicz and G. K. Dhaliwal (eds), *Going Straight: Effective Delinquency Prevention and Offender Rehabilitation*. Ottawa: Air Training and Publications.

Ross, R. R., and Fabiano, E. A. (1983). *The Cognitive Model of Crime and Delinquency Prevention and Rehabilitation: Intervention Techniques*. Ottawa: Ontario Ministry of Correctional Services.

Ross, R. R., Antonowicz, D. H., and Dhaliwal, G. K. (1995). *Going Straight: Effective Delinquency Prevention and Offender Rehabilitation*. Ottawa: Air Training and Publications.

Rotman, E. (1990). *Beyond Punishment: A New View of the Rehabilitation of Criminal Offenders*. Westport, Conn.: Greenwood Press.

Rumgay, J. (2004). Scripts for safer survival: Pathways out of female crime. *Howard Journal of Criminal Justice, 43*, 405–19.

Ryff, C. D., and Singer, B. (1998). The contours of positive human health. *Psychological Inquiry, 9*(1), 1–28.

Salekin, R. (2002). Psychopathy and therapeutic pessimism: Clinical lore or clinical reality? *Clinical Psychology Review, 22*, 79–112.

Salter, A. C. (1988). *Treating Child Sex Offenders and Their Victims: A Practical Guide*. Newbury Park, Calif.: Sage Publications.

Sampson, R. J., and Laub, J. (1993). *Crime in the Making: Pathways and Turning Points through Life*. Cambridge, Mass.: Harvard University Press.

Sampson, R. J., and Laub, J. (1997). A life-course theory of cumulative disadvantage and the stability of delinquency. *Advances in Criminological Theory*, 7, 133–61.

Schneider, K. J. (1999). Clients deserve relationships, not merely "treatments". *American Psychologist*, 54, 206–7.

Seligman, M. E. P. (2002). Positive psychology, positive prevention, and positive therapy. In C. R. Snyder and S. J. Lopez (eds), *Handbook of Positive Psychology*. New York: Oxford University Press.

Seligman, M. E. P., and Csikszentmihalyi, M. (2000). Positive psychology: An introduction. *American Psychologist*, 55, 5–14.

Seligman, M. E. P., and Peterson, C. (2003). Positive clinical psychology. In L. G. Aspinwall and U. M. Staudinger (eds), *A Psychology of Human Strengths: Fundamental Questions and Future Directions for a Positive Psychology*. Washington, DC: American Psychological Association.

Sennett, R. (2003). *Respect in a World of Inequality*. New York: Norton.

Serin, R., and Kennedy, S. (1997). Treatment readiness and responsivity: Contributing to effective correctional programming. *Research Report*, Correctional Services Canada.

Sherman, L. W. (1993). Defiance, deterrence, and irrelevance: A theory of the criminal sanction. *Journal of Research in Crime and Delinquency*, 30, 445–73.

Shover, N. (1996). *Great Pretenders: Pursuits and Careers of Persistent Thieves*. Boulder, Colo.: Westview Press.

Siegert, R., and Ward, T. (2007). Evolutionary theory and clinical psychology. In S. O. Lilienfeld and W. O'Donohue (eds), *The Great Ideas of Clinical Science: The 18 Concepts Every Mental Health Researcher and Practitioner Should Understand*. (pp. 243–261) Oxford: Routledge.

Simon, J. (1993). *Poor Discipline*. Chicago, Ill.: University of Chicago Press.

Singer, J. A. (2005). *Personality and Psychotherapy: Treating the Whole Person*. New York: Guilford Press.

Social Exclusion Unit (2001). *Reducing Re-offending by Ex-prisoners*. London: Home Office.

Sparks, R. (2001). Degrees of estrangement: The cultural theory of risk and comparative penology. *Theoretical Criminology*, 5, 159–76.

Stefanakis, H. (1998). *Desistence from Violence: Men's Stories of Identity Transformation*. Unpublished doctoral dissertation, University of Guelph, Canada.

Steiner, F. (2002). *Human Ecology: Following Nature's Lead*. Washington, DC: Island Press.

Sterelny, K. (2003). *Thought in a Hostile World: The Evolution of Human Cognition*. Oxford: Blackwell.

Sutherland, E., and Cressey, D. (1978). *Criminology*, 10th edn. New York: Lippincott.

Sutherland, Edwin (1947). *Principles of Criminology*, 4th edn. Philadelphia, Pa: Lippincott.

Terry, C. M. (2002). *The Fellas: Overcoming Prison and Addiction*. Belmont, Calif.: Wadsworth.

Theodossiou, I. (1997). The effects of low pay and unemployment on psychological well-being: A logistic regression approach. *Journal of Health Economics, 18,* 693–704.

Thompson, R. A. (1994). Emotional regulation: A theme in search of definition. In N. A. Fox (ed.), *The Development of Emotion Regulation: Biological and Behavioral Considerations*. Monographs of the Society for Research in Child Development, Vol. 59, Serial No. 240.

Thomson, G. (1987). *Needs*. London: Routledge & Kegan Paul.

Thornton, D. (2002) Constructing and testing a framework for dynamic risk assessment. *Sexual Abuse: A Journal of Research and Treatment, 14,* 139–54.

Toch, H. (1997). *Corrections: A Humanistic Approach*. Guilderland, NY: Harrow & Heston.

Toch, H. (2002). Everything works. *International Journal of Offender Therapy and Comparative Criminology, 46,* 119–22.

Toch, H., and Wilkins, L. (1985). Machine inferences and clinical judgments: A debate. *Criminal Justice and Behavior, 11,* 263–75.

Tomasello, M. (1999). *The Cultural Origins of Human Cognition*. Cambridge, Mass.: Harvard University Press.

Tong, L. S. J., and Farrington, D. P. (2006). How effective is the "Reasoning and Rehabilitation" programme in reducing reoffending?: A meta-analysis evaluation in four countries. *Psychology, Crime & Law, 12,* 3–24.

Tooby, J., and Cosmides, L. (1992). The psychological foundations of culture. In J. H. Barkow, L. Cosmides and J. Tooby (eds), *The Adapted Mind: Evolutionary Psychology and the Generation of Culture*. New York: Oxford

Trasler, G. B. (September 1980). *Aspects of Causality, Culture, and Crime*. Paper presented at the Fourth International Seminar at the International Centre of Sociological, Penal and Penitentiary Research and Studies, Messina, Italy.

Travis, J. (2000). *But They All Come Back: Rethinking Prisoner Reentry, Research in Brief – Sentencing and Corrections: Issues for the 21st Century* (NCJ 181413). Washington, DC: US Department of Justice, National Institute of Justice.

Travis, J. (2005). *But They All Come Back: Facing the Challenges of Prisoner Reentry*. New York: Urban Institute.

Visher, C. (2006). Effective reentry programs. *Criminology and Public Policy, 5,* 299–304.

Wade, D. T., and de Jong, B. A. (2000). Recent advances in rehabilitation. *British Medical Journal, 320,* 1385–8.

Ward, T., and Keenan, T. (1999). Child molesters' implicit theories. *Journal of Interpersonal Violence*, *14*(8), 821–38.

Ward, T., and Hudson, S. M. (2000). A self-regulation model of relapse prevention. In D. R. Laws, S. M. Hudson and T. Ward (eds), *Remaking Relapse Prevention with Sex Offenders: A Sourcebook*. Newbury Park, Calif.: Sage.

Ward, T., and Siegert, R. J. (2002). Toward a comprehensive theory of child sexual abuse: A theory knitting perspective. *Psychology, Crime & Law*, *9*, 319–51.

Ward, T., and Brown, M. (2003). The Risk–Need Model of offender rehabilitation: A critical analysis. In T. Ward, D. R. Laws and S. H. Hudson (eds), *Sexual Deviance: Issues and Controversies*. Thousand Oaks, Calif.: Sage.

Ward, T., and Stewart, C. (2003). Criminogenic needs and human needs: A theoretical model. *Psychology, Crime & Law*, *9*, 125–43.

Ward, T., and Brown, M. (2004). The Good Lives Model and conceptual issues in offender rehabilitation. *Psychology, Crime & Law*, *10*, 243–57.

Ward, T., and Marshall, W. L. (2004). Good lives, aetiology and the rehabilitation of sex offenders: A bridging theory. *Journal of Sexual Aggression: Special Issue: Treatment & Treatability*, *10*, 153–69.

Ward, T., and Gannon, T. (2006). Rehabilitation, etiology, and self-regulation: The Good Lives Model of sexual offender treatment. *Aggression and Violent Behavior*, *11*, 77–94.

Ward, T., and Yates, P. M. (2006). The rehabilitation of offenders: Integrating the Good Lives Model and the Risk Need Responsivity model. *Manuscript in preparation*.

Ward, T., Laws, D. R., and Hudson, S. H.(2003)(eds). *Sexual Deviance: Issues and Controversies*. Thousand Oaks, Calif.: Sage.

Ward, T., Bickley, J., Webster, S. D., Fisher, D., Beech, A., and Eldridge, H. (2004). *The Self-regulation Model of the Offense and Relapse Process: A Manual*, Vol. 1, *Assessment*. Victoria, BC: Pacific Psychological Assessment Corporation.

Ward, T., Polaschek, D., and Beech, A. R. (2006). *Theories of Sexual Offending*. Chichester: John Wiley.

Ward, T., Yates, P. M., and Long, C. A. (2006). *The Self-Regulation Model of the Offence and Re-offence Process*, Vol. 2, *Treatment*. Victoria, BC: Pacific Psychological Assessment Corporation.

Ward, T., Gannon, T., and Mann, R. (2007). The Good Lives Model of offender rehabilitation: Clinical implications. *Aggression and Violent Behavior*, *12*, 87–107.

Warr, M. (2002). *Companions in Crime*. Cambridge: Cambridge University Press.

Warren, M. Q. (1969). The case for differential treatment of delinquents. *Annals of the American Academy of Political and Social Science*, *381*, 47–59.

White, W. L. (1998). *Slaying the Dragon: The History of Addiction Treatment and Recovery in America*. Bloomington, Ind.: Chestnut Health Systems.

Whitehead, P., Ward, T., and Collie, R. (in press). Time for a change: Applying the Good Lives Model of rehabilitation to a high-risk violent offender. *International Journal of Offender Therapy and Comparative Criminology*.

Wiggins, J. S. (1991). Agency and communion as conceptual coordinates for the understanding and measurement of interpersonal behavior. In D. Cicchetti and W. Grove (eds), *Thinking Clearly about Psychology*. Minneapolis, Minn.: University of Minnesota.

Wilson, D. B., Bouffard, L. A., and MacKenzie, D. L. (2005). A quantitative review of structured, group-oriented, cognitive-behavioral programs for offenders. *Criminal Justice and Behavior, 32*, 172–204.

Wilson, J. A., and Davis, R. C. (2006). Good intentions meet hard realities: An evaluation of the Project Greenlight Reentry Program. *Criminology and Public Policy, 5*, 303–38.

Wilson, W. J., and Neckerman, K. M. (1987). Poverty and family structure: The widening gap between evidence and public policy issues. In S. H. Danziger and D. H. Weinberg (eds), *Fighting Poverty: What Works and What Doesn't*. Cambridge, Mass.: Harvard University Press.

Wrzesniewski, A., Roszin, P., and Bennett, G. (2003). Working, playing, and eating: Making the most of most moments. In C. L. M. Keyes and J. Haidt (eds), *Flourishing: Positive Psychology and the Life Well-lived*. Washington, DC: American Psychological Association.

Yates, P. M. (2003). Treatment of adult sexual offenders: A therapeutic cognitive-behavioral model of intervention. *Journal of Child Sexual Abuse, 12*, 195–232.

Yates, P. M., Goguen, B. C., Nicholaichuk, T. P., Williams, S. M., Long, C. A., Jeglic, E., and Martin, G. (2000). *National Sex Offender Programs (Moderate, Low, and Maintenance Intensity Levels)*. Ottawa: Correctional Service of Canada.

Young, J. (1999). *The Exclusive Society: Social Exclusion, Crime and Difference in Late Modernity*. London: Sage Publications.

INDEX